ETHNIC CONFLICT
AND TERRORISM

This book aims to understand the origin and dynamics of so-called intranational conflicts such as those that have been affecting Europe (Northern Ireland, the Basque Country region in Spain, Corsica in France, the former Yugoslavia and Albania), and a number of countries in the developing world (Rwanda, Liberia, Sierra Leone, Sudan and Uganda, Haiti, India, Pakistan and others) and how these conflicts have been invested by terrorist organisations at both national and international levels.

To analyse their emergence and development, the book offers an introduction into nine basic mechanisms analysed and defined by social sciences disciplines such as sociology, anthropology, political sciences and social psychology, that are relevant to the understanding of these conflicts. The nine themes are divided into two groups: long-term macro issues and short-term micro issues and each chapter analyses one of these mechanisms or themes. Ultimately this book defines a number of considerations aiming at the development of policies to prevent and stop such conflicts.

This book will be of interest to undergraduates and post-graduate students in conflict and terrorism studies.

Joseph L. Soeters is Professor of Organization Studies and Social Sciences at the Royal Netherlands Military Academy and Tilburg University. His research interests mainly focus on international military co-operation and societal developments in the Western and non-Western world. He has published in excess of 155 articles and chapters in edited volumes and (co-)edited five books, both in Dutch and English. He is involved with projects in Eritrea, Bolivia and the Baltic states. He is also Vice-President of the Research Committee 'Armed Forces and Conflict Resolution' of the International Sociological Association.

CONTEMPORARY SECURITY STUDIES

ETHNIC CONFLICT AND TERRORISM

The Origins and Dynamics of Civil Wars

Joseph L. Soeters

Routledge
Taylor & Francis Group

LONDON AND NEW YORK

First published 2005
by Routledge
2 Park Square, Milton Park, Abingdon,
Oxon OX14 4RN

Simultaneously published in the USA and Canada
by Routledge
270 Madison Ave, New York, NY 10016

Routledge is an imprint of the Taylor & Francis Group

© 2005 Joseph L. Soeters

Typeset in Times by Keyword Group
Printed and bound in Great Britain by TJ International Ltd,
Padstow, Cornwall

British Library Cataloguing in Publication Data
A catalogue record for this book is available from the British Library

Library of Congress Cataloging in Pubication Data
Soeters, J.
Ethnic conflict and terrorism: the origins and dynamics of civil wars/
Joseph L. Soeters.
p. cm.
Includes bibliographical references and index.
ISBN 0-415-36587-2 (hardback) – ISBN 0-415-36588 (pbk) 1.
Ethnic conflict. 2. Intergroup relations. 3. Violence. 4. Civil war.
5. Terrorism.
I. Title.
HM1121.S64 2005
303.6`2´089—dc22   2005004829

Hardback ISBN: 0-415-36587-2
Paperback ISBN: 0-415-36588-0

CONTENTS

PREFACE

In 1994, I started giving lectures in social sciences at the Royal Netherlands Military Academy. In those years Western societies and their armed forces were confronted with an unexpected upheaval of violence in the world. The Cold War had come to an end and paradoxically, Western armed forces were called upon to bring stability and peace in various conflict regions around the world. Somalia, Rwanda and Bosnia had rather suddenly become well-known names.

No longer accustomed to real life hostilities, the Western militaries deployed missions that, in the beginning, were not very successful. The United States started to pull back its troops from Somalia after having suffered unexpectedly high numbers of casualties. So did the Belgians in Rwanda, a country where appalling killing stupefied a UN mission commanded by a Canadian general. In 1995, the Dutch military witnessed the largest human slaughter in Europe since the Second World War in the Srebrenica Valley in Bosnia. Clearly, Western societies and their militaries were not prepared mentally for the task they were set to do. There was simply no emotional or rational understanding of the incredible events that were taking place simultaneously in so many places around the world. And yet, the military were expected to make a difference in preventing, containing and solving this type of intranational strife. Hence, I made the decision to use this type of internal strife as a starting point for a course in general social sciences at the Royal Netherlands Military Academy.

Not much later, when the new millennium had only just begun, terrorism struck. Whenever 9/11 is mentioned, no further clarification is needed. This date in 2001 has become historical. Since then, very violent attacks have occurred in Bali in Indonesia, Casablanca in Morocco, Riyadh in Saudi Arabia, Istanbul in Turkey, as well as in Madrid in continental Europe. In addition, Russia especially has witnessed a number of gruesome events causing the killing of hundreds of people in each incident. These events are directly related to the Chechen War. Again, all this affects the Western militaries since they have been assigned to fight the 'war on terror' and to intervene in unstable regions, such as Afghanistan, where terrorism and ethnicity-related conflicts flourish. Concurrently, in the African continent, many extremely violent internal conflicts are raging which the West would rather wish to ignore but which beg our attention. Clearly, some ten years after my first lectures, the course is as relevant and topical as ever before.

This small book contains the essence of the course. It was originally intended for student-officers, but a number of experiences have demonstrated that students in history, international relations, economics and social sciences may profit from its content as well. So may a more broadly interested readership that wants to understand the horrifying incidents that one can read about in the daily papers. If this book contributes to a somewhat better understanding of what is taking place, or to the awareness and skills to prevent the violence, however small and insignificant, then it has reached its goal.

ACKNOWLEDGEMENTS

This book has grown over the years. Two previous editions (1997 and 2004) have been published in the Dutch language. The current English edition is an upgraded and expanded version incorporating new theoretical insights and empirical findings. While drafting these editions many people have helped me with their comments, their willingness to make me aware of even more literature and with checking the manuscript for mistakes and inconsistencies. In chronological order, I would like to thank Rudy Richardson, Axel Rosendahl Huber, Wim Klinkert, Boris Timmer, Ger Teitler, Joris van Bladel, Ruud Grothausen, Vivian Schreurs, Coen van den Berg, Ad Vogelaar, Peter Olsthoorn, Luciella Boeddha, Alisa Hozo, Nives Elez, Fleur Soeters, Geesje Bos, Eric Franken, Geert Hofstede, Cor Lammers, Andrew Humphrys and Andrew Baxter.

Harry Kirkels and Alexander Alta translated the Dutch manuscript into beautiful English. In updating the translated text, I received invaluable support from my close colleagues Rene Moelker and Robert-Jan Smits. Arzu Wasti in Istanbul encouraged me to produce this English version of the book and during the process, helped me with sound advice. Marjorie Francois gave good assistance and wonderful support whenever needed.

'We do not fully understand the conditions under which a civilising process moves into "reverse gear".'

Dunning, 1988

'The process of civilisation is a sustained attempt to regulate murderous urges.'

de Swaan, 1993

'That same day the last Belgian blue helmets leave Rwanda in a *Blitz*-evacuation they themselves referred to as "Out of Africa". Their commanders do not react when on arriving home in Brussels the soldiers cut their berets to ribbons in front of the cameras'.

de Temmerman, 1994

'Ethnic conflict is caused by the fear of the future, lived through the past.'

Pesic, 1994

'I could never understand why ten years ago my mother every now and then said with a sigh, "I wish there is not going to be war, everything is just fine as long as there is not going to be war"'.

Ugresic, 1995

'A state spilling blood to crush *Jihad* creates the conditions for the next *Jihad*.'

Goudsmit, 1995

'A tree trunk does not change into a crocodile just because it has been in the water for some time. Likewise, a Tutsi will always be a Tutsi, with his or her malice, deviousness and dishonesty.'

Bossema, 1996

'They put a weapon into your hands and say, "Shoot, there's your enemy!" Imagine, one bullet costs three Deutsch Marks — that is one life. Imagine: three Marks, one man.'

Faber, 2001

'To comprehend the tragic events of 9/11, we first need to acquire (...) an answer to the question, why do people behave the way they do.'

Pyszczynski et al., 2002[1]

[1]The first quote is from Eric Dunning and can be found in Bax, M., *Medjugorje: Religion, Politics, and Violence in Rural Bosnia,* VU University Press, Amsterdam, 101, 1995. The second quotation is the conclusion of an interview that Ramdas, A. had with de Swaan, A., published in Ramdas, A., *In mijn vaders huis (In My Father's House),* Mets, Amsterdam, 41, 1993. The third quotation is from de Temmerman, E., *De doden zijn niet dood. Rwanda, een ooggetuigenverslag (The Dead are not Dead. Rwanda, an Eyewitness Report),* Arbeiderspers, Amsterdam, 33, 1994. The fourth quotation is attributed to Vesna Pesic and can be found in Lake, D.A. and Rothchild, D., Containing fear. The origins and management of ethnic conflict, *International Security,* 21, 41–75, 1996. The fifth quotation is from Dubravka Ugresic, *De cultuur van leugens (The Culture of Lies),* Nijgh & Van Ditmar, Amsterdam, 12, 1995. The sixth quote is from Goudsmit, G., *Anatomie van de FIS terreur* (Anatomy of the FIS-terror), *Volkskrant,* 5, 4 April 1995. The seventh quotation is from Bossema, W., *Boomstronk wordt geen krokodil* (Tree-stump does not become a crocodile), *Volkskrant,* 5, 7 November 1996. The eighth quotation is from Faber, M., *Novi Dani, nieuwe dagen. Oorlog en biografie in Banja Luka, Bosnië-Herzegovina (Novi Dani, New Days. War and Biography in Banja Luka, Bosnia-Hercegovina),* Aksant, Amsterdam, 101, 2001. The final citation is from Pyszczynski, T., Solomon, S. and Greenberg, J., *In the Wake of 9/11. The Psychology of Terror,* APA, Washington DC, 11, 2003.

1

INTRODUCTION

How could it have come to this? To what depths can one sink? How, in God's name, is this possible? These and comparable phrases express the despair of those who have been confronted with the images of erupting violence in Somalia, the Congo, Bosnia, Kosovo, Chechnya, the Moluccans, Haiti, Afghanistan and Iraq over the past few years. They are words of bewilderment uttered by people who have come to know about the murderous actions in Algeria, the Sudan, India, Sri Lanka, Bolivia or South Africa, words of those who see on their TV screens how Palestinian suicide squads cause death and destruction in the streets of Jerusalem or Tel Aviv or how 'infant soldiers' toting machine guns terrorise the streets of Monrovia in Liberia. And, naturally, on 11 September 2001, there was widespread bewilderment at seeing two hijacked airplanes crash into the Twin Towers in New York, resulting in just under three thousand dead.

It is not easy to get a rational grip on these attacks against the social order and human co-existence. For that is what they are: these atrocities that are the result of internal civil wars, ethnic rivalry, mob attacks, insurgencies, revolts and terrorism. The main question that remains is how this kind of violence could have come about. It is just a matter of good fortune that this question can easily and almost carelessly be brushed aside. After all, in most cases these orgies of violence occur at considerable distance from our own backyard. Moreover, they are transitory and temporary phenomena.

However, that is not all there is to it. The German essay writer Enzensberger has put the violence occurring in 'outer areas' on the same line with a global change of mentality, which must inevitably lead to a war of 'all against all'. He found support in this from Mestrovic, a sociologist from the former Yugoslavia, who predicted the 'Balkanisation of the West', if we are not careful. Earlier, the French political scientist de Guéhenno spoke of the approaching 'Lebanisation of the world', when he referred to the imminent war between one community and another, using the example of the previously peaceful city of Beirut in Lebanon exploding into violence during the 1970s and 1980s.[1] Perhaps these authors were overly pessimistic — Beirut, for instance, has currently regained its former status of the 'Paris of the Middle East'[2] — but their warnings carry at least one implication, namely that the question as to why these violent actions take place should by no means leave us unconcerned. There are at least three good reasons for that.

The first reason to be concerned about violence is its ubiquity. It takes place close to home, much closer than we tend to think at first hand. The incessant 'everyday' violence in the Basque province and Northern Ireland, where British soldiers are still gaining much 'practical experience', should make that clear. In Corsica, separatist bombers have succeeded in scaring away tourists and investors from this Ile de Beauté.[3] Disturbances in Cyprus between the Turkish and Greek inhabitants intermittently flare up, necessitating the presence of thousands of foreign soldiers to ensure restraint. Globalisation, too, has an effect on the rise of violence and conflict. Due to worldwide terrorism there is no place that is really safe anymore — attacks happen all over the world (in Bali, Istanbul, Moscow, New York, Washington, Casablanca, Madrid and other hotspots) and this is not likely to change in the near future.

Secondly, violence is definitely not a passing phenomenon. Conflicts follow one after the other, wave after wave. The genocide in Rwanda in 1994 was immediately followed up in neighbouring countries such as Burundi and the Congo. When the Tsunami-flooding in the Far East shocked the world during Christmas 2004, the killings in the Congo continued to cause the loss of tens of people a day. The problems in Somalia were only just abating when the Sudan was moving towards an expanding war. Although the Northern and Southern parties in Sudan signed a peace treaty in the beginning of 2005, the cruel hostilities in the Western part of the country (Darfur) have not ceased. In Afghanistan, a certain level of tranquillity has only just returned whereas neighbouring Tajikistan, the papers report, has disintegrated and now only consists of armed factions.[4] In Bosnia, the worst problems seem to be under control due to the presence of the international peace contingent, but after Bosnia came Kosovo and the violent upheavals in Albania and Macedonia, not to mention the situation that has arisen in Iraq since 2003. Even in peaceful Thailand, violent confrontations between the armed forces and secessionist protesters from the South have led to some 450 deaths in the course of 2004.

The final reason is that violence cannot be accepted morally. If ever violence were morally acceptable, then it is not so in this case. This type of violence belongs to the category of so-called 'unjust wars', wars that cannot be justified either morally or legally. There is no possible way in which the violence in these conflicts can be looked upon as the last resort in furthering a just cause. When there are victims, no distinction is made between the civilian population (who are raped, maimed and massacred) and the 'regular' fighters, the soldiers. What is more, there is no cause that can ever justify either the killing of almost 800,000 people, as happened in Rwanda in the first half of 1994, or the death of some 3.5 million people in the Congo since 1998. There is nothing that can legitimise the expulsion or displacement of hundreds of thousands of people, which occurs in almost every civil war.[5] In the conflicts of today there is no proportion whatsoever between the number of casualties and victims on the one hand and the political or military goals pursued on the other. These are absolute conflicts without rules or conventions, without the least respect of one human towards another.[6]

It is for these reasons that I want to try and answer the question about the origins and dynamics of violence and conflict from a sociological perspective. Here and there, I shall cast my proverbial net into the more distant waters of the social sciences, in particular in the abundant fishing grounds of anthropology, political science and social psychology. Arguments in the domain of individual psychology and psychiatry, however, lie outside the scope of my efforts.

It must certainly be true that every human being has an innate tendency towards aggression. It is also quite possible that brain deficiencies or youth traumas enhance aggression and violent behaviour, but these considerations shall be left untouched in this present study. Nor shall I draw comparisons with the animal world. There are ample indications that violence among animals is of a more limited and individualistic nature, lasts less long and is more 'target-oriented' than the atrocities which violence among humans may lead to. The relevance, therefore, of these kinds of comparisons appear to be minimal. Collins, the sociologist whose name will surface a number of times, has come up with a telling formulation for this: 'Human fighting does not reflect our animal heritage, but is rather a cultural achievement which overcomes that heritage. And indeed, human battlefields are notable for the way animal life quickly flees from them.'[7] This book is about violence as collective social behaviour or, to quote van Doorn and Hendrix, 'the violent clash between organized complexes of man and means, prepared and set for collective annihilation'. In this, individual personal aggression is an attendant phenomenon at most, not an explanatory one.[8]

I shall concentrate on the violence as it is caused and suffered by 'ordinary humans'. Consequently, my primary focus is not on the 'conduct' of states, as it already features largely in polemology, the study of international relations and historical macro-sociology. Strategic political considerations with respect to interstate relations are not included in this treatise, which instead deals with 'ordinary' violence inside states, or what is left of them.

It concerns violence of groups of people towards other groups within a state, often referred to as ethnic rivalry or conflicts, or violence between (segments of) the population and the central government, whether firmly in place or waning. In the latter case, we speak of so-called insurgencies, revolutions and guerrillas (also known as small wars), or the smaller scale, but equally effective, terrorist movements. They do not necessarily always target their own governments directly. As the 11 September 2001 attacks have shown, terrorist acts can also be aimed at a foreign power which, in the eyes of the perpetrators, has too much influence on their own government. Likewise, as the attacks of November 2003 against the synagogues and the British consulate in Istanbul made clear, they can be directed at a group in another country that has to be 'fought' or 'punished'. It should also be noted that ethnic groups in conflict sometimes spread across state boundaries, which implies that ethnic rivalry often has international dimensions. In addition, many conflicts are instigated and heated up by influences from outside the country. In the current globalising world nothing remains really internal.[9]

Fortunately, civil conflicts and uprisings do not always entail the use of violence, which means to say — the demonstration of power deliberately aimed at physically and mentally harming people as well as their temporary or permanent subjection. Perfect examples of conflicts without violence are the so-called 'velvet' or 'silent revolutions', which took place in various Eastern European countries in 1989 and 1990. In countries such as former East Germany, Hungary and Poland, and in 2004 during the 'Orange Revolution' in the Ukraine, the population took to the streets to demonstrate against their central governments. Apart from the odd incident, this successful struggle took place almost without violence, which is remarkable, to say the least.[10]

Many other conflicts are developing now, as they did in the past, with a lot more violence. Examples are conflicts among groups within the population, as occurred in Cambodia in the 1970s, resulting in more than 1.5 million people being killed, and in the former Yugoslavia, where during the 1990s, about 200,000 people died as a consequence of internal strife. Other conflicts are between the people and the central government. Examples are the Chechen war of independence (1990s) and the struggle of the Kurds in Turkey (1970s–1990s), or, in the distant past, the resistance of Indonesian groups against Dutch colonial rule (1945–1950) and currently, the rebellion in Aceh against Indonesia's central government. It should be noted that in these latter conflicts, the central governments and their armed forces often used considerable violence against the rebelling population groups. Hence, intranational violence comes as much from above as from below. The current acts of fury in the Congo are a mixture. They are manifestations of a struggle not only against the government, but also of a struggle amongst groups of the population themselves. Such collective acts of violence may develop in a more or less co-ordinated way and cause harm, to a greater or lesser extent, to society. The greater the advance planning and co-ordination, the greater is the damage to society.[11]

All in all, I am trying to make use of a broad social-scientific perspective in the exploration of the origin and dynamics of conflict and violence within the state, which implies that I shall be looking for the general, as opposed to the specific. In this book, the wide angle lens is used and there is no zooming in on details, however significant they may be in themselves. I shall be looking for the general mechanisms and processes one is bound to come across in the search for an explanation of violence and conflict. This concerns social phenomena, not the laws of natural science. Social mechanisms have the character of probability: when 'x' occurs, it is probable but not necessary that 'y' will also occur. These kinds of social phenomena or mechanisms are less forceful than the laws of natural science, but they offer significantly more than just a description of every separate case.[12]

It speaks for itself that in the analysis of real outbreaks of violence, additional facts and analyses have to be consulted. For impressive descriptions of the backgrounds and events during the conflicts in Bosnia, Rwanda, the Congo and Chechnya, mention must be made of the books of journalists such as Glenny, Rieff, Silber and Little, Ugresic, de Temmerman, Gourevitch, Hatzfeld, Joris and Bennett. They were there and gave eyewitness accounts. These books and other, more academic writings shall be referred to regularly in what follows.[13] Although I will focus relatively more on Rwanda and Bosnia, the examples I will use in this book come from all parts of the world.

The world in motion

There are good reasons to focus our attention on the 'violence of the ordinary human being'. The first reason is simply that 'ordinary violence' increased considerably, especially in the 1990s. The number of armed conflicts rose from 47 to 55 in the period between 1989 and 1992, mainly due to the increase of the so-called small armed conflicts (low-intensity wars). Almost 30 of the armed conflicts at that time could be typified as civil wars. Particularly in Europe and Africa, a remarkable rise in the number of relatively small intranational or intrastate conflicts could be seen.

This type of conflict has a toll of numerous deaths and refugees every year. According to the World Health Organization, each year, an estimated 500,000 people die in acts of (internal) war; over the past few years these casualties have mainly occurred in Africa. Intrastate conflicts are becoming relatively more important than the traditional interstate wars, both where frequency and the impact on society are concerned. It is true that intranational conflicts have a tendency to occur more frequently and cause more casualties than conflicts between nations. This trend started in the 1950s and, more prominently, after 1975. It is not without reason that the twentieth century is called the 'age of genocide'. But time goes on. The most recent years after 1992 show a reduction of the number of conflicts, intranationally as well as internationally. In 1995 and later, 'only' some 35 armed conflicts could be counted (most of them being internal), which indicates a certain stabilisation during the turbulent period immediately after the

Cold War. However, the phenomenon of violent conflicts involving 'ordinary people', or rather the so-called 'New Wars', continues to force itself upon us almost every day, especially because of their gruesome nature.[14]

At an early stage, the rise and background of these intrastate conflicts were observed by historian Martin van Creveld and by political scientist Samuel Huntington. The latter pointed out that conflicts since the Cold War have more often had a cultural, ethnic and religious nature and less often a political nature, as is the case with conflicts within (former) states and interstate conflicts, respectively. What ensued after the collapse of the Berlin Wall, therefore, is not a warless society, as many believed, but rather a condition of fragmenting peace. Since the disappearance of the *Pax Atomica* — the balance of power between the US and the former Soviet Union — and the demise of the *Pax Sovietica*, there is room for pressure from the bottom. This means that there is room for groups of people and regional movements, which generally have no difficulty arming themselves, striving for autonomy.[15]

As was observed earlier, the phenomenon of ethnic or communal violence has developed over many decades. From the decolonisation period onward, ethnic conflicts have contained 'elements of universality and uniformity that were not present at earlier times'.[16] Then, during the decolonisation of the 1940s, 1950s and 1960s, a first wave of restructuring took place, especially in Asia and Africa. Latin America witnessed continual internal strife during the 1970s and 1980s (El Salvador, Chile, Columbia, Peru), but those countries managed to solve these problems, at least to some extent and for some time.[17] In the 1990s, the pressure from the bottom grew stronger again, especially in Europe, Africa and the Caucasus. Now, a second round of restructuring or reorganisation crisis seems to be taking place, which has seemingly passed its culmination point of 1992, as we saw before. Still, there is no reason for unconcern.

The pressure towards autonomy and new mutual relationships is enhanced by the uncertainty about employment, prosperity and the environment. As a consequence of a rearranging world economy and growing pressure due to population growth, the self-certainty of these matters has become doubtful. Basic human needs, such as fresh water, fertile soil, fishing grounds and oil, continue to become increasingly scarce. Fresh water reserves, for example, are under strain. In certain parts of the world, their control is a source of rising tension. Too little water leads to increasing food scarcity, which, experts say, will polarise ethnic and regional opposition in a variety of places across the world. In general, low incomes are a major factor impacting on the development of internal strife and civil war, as has been demonstrated in a number of quantitative studies.[18]

Given the importance of economic factors, it comes as no surprise that part of the current ethnic and regional strife in regions such as the

Sudan, Chechnya and Nigeria is about the control of raw materials, in this case oil, or about diamonds in other parts of Africa, like Sierra Leone. The control of raw materials and civil wars often go hand in hand. This strife occurs because minority groups or central governments dispute the control, and hence the gains, of the raw materials. This has its worldwide impact — in the closing days of September 2004, ethnic upheaval in Nigeria targeting oil refineries led to an all time high record in the price of crude oil.[19]

Moreover, in connection with these economic factors, almost one-third of the working world population is completely or partially out of work and live on or below the poverty line. This disrupts societies, also because it causes a trek to large urban areas. Many a metropolis has more inhabitants than the entire population of the Netherlands, which is 16 million. This causes social uprooting but it does not mean that in the cities, these migrants can be certain of finding the work and prosperity they lack in rural areas. This results in the social exclusion of large numbers of people.[20] Sociological views say that this leads to atomising and the absence of norms — people adopt a more negative attitude and become more careless because of it. Generally speaking, this leads to a crushing of existing institutes and social relations. It is with reason that people refer to the end of organised capitalism and the rise of the 'risk society', a society from which existing patterns and certainties are disappearing.[21] As a consequence, people get scared and angry — the abbreviation USA has now even come to mean the United States of Anger for some.[22] However, anger and the search for new identities are not restricted to the USA.

Throughout the world people are looking for new certainties, new anchors and identities that put sense into their existence. Worldwide, cultural minorities such as indigenous people, national minorities and migrant groups are striving for emancipation, multicultural citizenship, equal rights, justice, educational facilities and opportunities to access the state's institutions. In South and Central America (Bolivia, Ecuador and Mexico), for instance, indigenous people ('Indians'), who form the majority of the population, are striving for the recognition of their own languages, access to educational facilities, as well as better job opportunities. In addition, they want to profit from the gains of the exploitation of natural gas in the country. Sometimes this leads to the use of (deadly) violence, both by rebellious groups and the state.[23] The revival of religion in Africa, South America, North America and also the Near and Far East, of course, must also be seen in connection with the search for (new) anchors and identities. Religion is important because it often promises a better life to the deprived. This religious revival may blend with political aims and indeed result in some people believing that they have to kill others for this.[24] One other effect of poverty atomising and the erosion of norms is that some people are attracted by 'easy money', the quickly-made riches gained by the production and dealing of drugs, diamonds and gold. The New Wars are often characterised by a mixture of political struggle and organised crime.[25]

There is still a final reason for observing the violence and therefore the behaviour of 'ordinary people' instead of the 'conduct of states' or the 'higher politics'. At the end of the day, the governance of states is invariably the work of humans. All conflicts, no matter what, are started by people of flesh and blood; ordinary people who have worked their way up to the level of the social, political and military elite of their country or region. Many macro-processes of order and conflict ultimately have a micro-sociological foundation — actual behaviour, direct interactions between people and emotions such as fear, jealousy, ambition, shame, frustration and anger. Without micro-processes, there are no conflicts.[26]

Nine mechanisms and processes

What follows has modest pretences. It is not an all-encompassing theory leading to hypotheses that can be tested, or to a complete model. It is more a collection of bits and pieces emerging from social-scientific literature, which can be linked to the origin of conflict and violence. As such, this book is of a positively introductory nature. Secondly, it is not meant to propose recipes for preventing or allaying outbursts of violence. If only it were that easy! Finally, much of what follows here must be familiar to the reader, either by personal observation and reflection, or through newspaper reports or TV documentaries. Perhaps not everything, and certainly not the complexity of factors, is self-evident. That must be where the benefit of this text lies.

I distinguish nine patterns of collective development and behaviour or, to put it differently, nine social mechanisms and processes that impact on the origin and dynamics of civil wars and violence. There will be partial overlap between these nine mechanisms and processes and generally, they operate in combination. Although these social phenomena can be unravelled analytically and theoretically, in reality, these factors are a jumble of causes and effects that refuse to be disentangled. Besides, these ever-changing combinations of causes lead to various types of violence. In other words, every actual outburst of violence has its own composition where the extent and the (combination of) causes of violence are concerned. So, every case is unique, yet generalities may be found. These are the nine social phenomena which can be referred to as mechanisms and processes leading to internal war, conflict and violence. The nine mechanisms and processes can schematically be divided into two categories — the macro and the micro level, as shown in Figure 1.[27]

The *macro level* implies large-scale processes that engulf entire continents and therefore involve large numbers of people. The smallest analysis unit

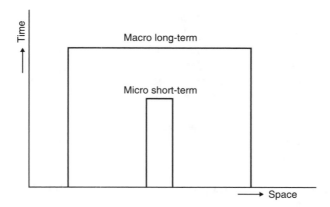

Figure 1 Schematic representation of macro and micro processes. Source: Collins, R., On the microfoundations of macrosociology, *American Journal of Sociology*, 86, 984–1014, 1981.

at macro level is generally the nation state. Moreover, macro processes cover the long term, centuries or — now that global developments seem to take place more quickly due to new technologies — at least some years or decades. Processes at micro level, on the other hand, take place in concrete interactions between humans and are, therefore, of a shorter duration. Micro processes develop over a number of years, but usually last only a couple of months, weeks or days. Normally, the number of participants involved in micro processes is relatively small but with the assistance of modern communication media, those micro processes occurring in speeches, facial expressions, power of persuasion and the like, can have a much wider impact. In the CNN era of today, images of an orating political leader are broadcast on live television the world over. Exactly because of this contemporary effect, the results of processes at both levels constantly interact, even to such an extent that the distinction between macro and micro seems somewhat artificial. Macro factors have a strong influence on micro behaviour, as they are the foundation or the seed-bed of events at the micro level but, conversely, micro factors may also lead to effects at macro level. The distinction between macro and micro must therefore be used with great care.

Five macro mechanisms and processes are used as background processes:

- Grid characteristics and group boundaries
- Waning government, democratic deficit and strategic constellation
- Violence and (de-)civilisation
- Violence and culture
- Rationalisation of evil

The four micro mechanisms and processes refer to:

- Group cohesion, stereotyping and ideologies
- Social mobilisation and leadership
- Rising expectations, relative deprivation and reduction of power distance
- The dynamics of the conflict itself

These nine mechanisms and processes will be discussed in just as many chapters. There is a fair comparison between the list of factors and what other authors have called the necessary preconditions of intranational, internal violence. However, in most other analyses, the main emphasis lies on the micro mechanisms and processes whereas in general, there is little or no emphasis on the breeding ground of conflicts, i.e. the macro mechanisms and processes.[28] A final chapter with a number of considerations for the prevention and solution of violent conflict concludes the book. An analysis of the mechanisms and processes leading to violence and conflict must necessarily also contain an understanding of the causes of the opposite situation, i.e. the absence of violence and conflict.

Notes

1. Enzensberger, H. M., *Oog in oog met de burgeroorlog (Eye to Eye with Civil War)*, De Bezige Bij, Amsterdam, 1994; Mestrovic, M., *The Balkanization of the West. The Confluence of Postmodernism and Postcommunism*, Routledge, London, 1994; de Guéhenno, J.M., *La Fin de la Démocratie (The End of Democracy)*, Editions Flammarion, Paris, 1993.
2. Kifner, J., Rich Arabs rediscover Paris of the Middle East, *New York Times*, 9 October 2004.
3. For instance, Poletti, J. G., *et al., Combien ça coute la violence*? (How much does this violence cost?) in *Corsica, Mensuel d'Information*, 16–24, October 2003.
4. See Tishkov, V., Ethnic conflicts in the former USSR: the use and misuse of typologies and data, *Journal of Peace Research*, 36, 571–591, 1999; About Afghanistan, see Misra, A., *Afghanistan. The Labyrinth of Violence*, Polity Press, Cambridge, 2004.
5. For instance, C. Kaufmann, Possible and impossible solutions to ethnic civil war, *International Security*, 20, 136–175, 1996, page 149 ff.
6. In civil wars in particular, the principles of discrimination and the proportional use of violence are trampled underfoot. See Walzer, M., *Just and Unjust Wars. A Moral Argument with Historical Illustrations*, Basic Books, New York, 1992; Teitler, G., *Toepassing van geweld. Sociologische essays over geweld, verzet en militaire organisatie (The Use of Violence. Sociological Essays on Violence, Resistance and Military Organization)*, Boom, Meppel, 19, 1972. For a description of the appalling experiences of many women during the war in the former Yugoslavia, see Allen, B., *Rape Warfare. The Hidden Genocide in Bosnia-Hercegovina and Croatia*, University of Minnesota Press, Minneapolis, 1996.

7. The comparisons with violence among animals can be found in Collins, R., *Gewelddadig conflict en sociale organisatie. Enkele theoretische implicaties van de sociologie van de oorlog (Violent conflict and social organization. Some theoretical implications of the sociology of war)*, Amsterdams Sociologisch Tijdschrift, 16, 63–87, 1990. An interesting study about monkeys is given in de Waal, F., *Good Natured. The Origins of Right and Wrong in Humans and Other Animals*, Harvard University Press, Cambridge, 1996. In this study, the author points at, in principle, the good-natured climate in which the monkeys live. Monkeys do not use physical violence against one another. de Waal, therefore, does not speak of the 'survival of the fittest' but of the 'survival of the kindest'.

8. van Doorn, J.A.A. and Hendrix, W.J., *Ontsporing van geweld. Over het Nederlands – Indisch – Indonesisch conflict (Derailment of Violence. About the Dutch-Indonesian-Dutch Conflict)*, Universitaire Pers Rotterdam, Rotterdam, especially pages 172–173, 1970.

9. Tishkov, V., op. cit., 576, 1999.

10. For a reflection about, and extensive definitions of violence the reader is referred to Popitz, H., *Phänomene der Gewalt (Manifestations of Violence)*, J.C.B. Mohr, Tübingen, 1999. An analysis of the 'velvet' revolutions in Eastern Europe in the early 1990s can be found in Arts, W., *Van fluwelen en stille revoluties (About Velvet and Silent Revolutions)*, inaugural lecture, Tilburg University, 1996.

11. For the Chechen war of independence, see for instance, Tishkov, V., *Chechnya: Life in a War-torn society*, University of California Press, Berkeley, 2004. For the Turkish internal conflicts see St. Kinzer, *Crescent and Star. Turkey between Two Worlds*, Farrar, Straus and Giroux, London and New York, 2001; Zürcher, E.J., *Turkey. A Modern History*, I.B. Tauris, London, 2004. The Indonesian uprising against Dutch colonial rule is described in van Doorn J.A.A. and Hendrix, W.J., op. cit., 1970; the current armed rebellion in Aceh is analysed in Aquino Siapno, J., *Gender, Islam, Nationalism and the State in Aceh. The Paradox of Power, Co-optation and Resistance*, RoutledgeCurzon, London, 2002. The internal conflicts in the Congo are engagingly described in Joris, L., *De dans van de luipaard (The Dance of the Leopard)*, Meulenhof, Amsterdam, 2001. The impact of various types of violence is analysed in Tilly, Ch., *The Politics of Collective Violence*, Cambridge UP, Cambridge, 14–15, 2003.

12. See for instance, Elster, J., *Nuts and Bolts for the Social Sciences*, Cambridge UP, Cambridge, 1993; or Coleman, J.S., *Foundations of Social Theory*, Belknap Press, Cambridge, 1994. For an explicit analysis of the differences between mechanisms and processes with respect to conflicts and contention, see also McAdam, D., *et al., The Dynamics of Contention*, Cambridge UP, Cambridge, 23–28, 2001.

13. For the former Yugoslavia, see Glenny, M., *The Fall of Yugoslavia*, Penguin Books, London, 1993; Rieff, D., *Slaughterhouse. Bosnia and the failure of the West*, Vintage, London, 1995; Silber, L. and Little, A., *The Death of Yugoslavia*, Penguin Books, London, 1996; Ugresic, D., *De cultuur van leugens (The Culture of Lies)*, Nijgh & Van Ditmar, Amsterdam, 1995; Duijzings, G.,

Geschiedenis en herinnering in Oost-Bosnië (History and Memory in Eastern Bosnia), Boom, Amsterdam, 2002. About Rwanda, de Temmerman, E., *De doden zijn niet dood. Rwanda, een ooggetuigenverslag (The Dead are not dead. An Eyewitness Report)*, Arbeiderspers, Amsterdam, 1994; Gourevitch, Ph., *We Wish to Inform You that Tomorrow We will be Killed with our Families*, Farrar, Straus and Giroux, New York, 1998; Hatzfeld, J., *Une saison des machettes (A Season of Machetes)*, Editions du Seuil, Paris, 2003. About Congo, see Joris, L., op. cit., 2001. For a description of the internal conflict in Algeria, see Labat, S., L' *Algérie dans la guerre (Algeria in War)* (ed.), Complex, Paris, 1994; an account of the armed forces' behaviour in that country is given in Saouida, H., *La sale guerre (The Dirty War)*, La Découverte, Paris, 2001. A description of the 'killing fields' in the Sudan is to be found in Millard Burr J. and Collins, Robert O., *Requiem for the Sudan — War, Drought and Disaster Relief on the Nile*, Westview Press, San Francisco, 1996; Scroggins, D., *Emma's War*, Pantheon Books, New York, 2002. A wealth of information on the multifaceted strife in Southern Asia can be found in Tambiah, S.J., *Leveling Crowds, Ethnonationalist Conflicts and Collective Violence in South Asia*, University of Calfiornia Press, Berkely, 1996. For descriptions of the Chechen war see Bennett, V., *Crying Wolf. The Return of War to Chechnya (updated ed.)*, Pan Books, London, 2001; Winslow D. and Moelker, R., Chechnya, caught between globalisation from above and globalisation from below, in Kooiman, D., *et al.* (eds.), *Conflicts in a Globalising World, Essays in Honour of Peter Kloos*, van Gorcum, Assen, 211–228, 2002. Descriptions and analyses of armed conflicts can be found in the regular publications of the Human Rights Watch as well as in the annual surveys published by the International Institute for Strategic Studies. An additional publication with a survey of ethnic disputes is Coakly, J. (ed.), *The Territorial Management of Ethnic Conflict*, 2nd and rev. edn, Frank Cass, London, 2003.

14. The 20th century has been indicated as the 'age of genocide' in Power, S., *A problem from hell. America and the age of genocide*, Basic Books, New York, 2002. See also Zwaan, T., *Civilisering en deciviliserings. Studies over staatsvorming en geweld, nationalisme en vervolging (Civilization and Decivilization. Studies on State Formation and Violence, Nationalism and Persecution)*, Boom, Amsterdam, 2001. For a more-or-less similar account see Mann, M., *The Dark side of Democracy: Explaining Ethnic Cleansing*, Cambridge UP, Cambridge, 2005. A survey of numbers of armed conflicts in the 1990s and later can be found in Wallensteen, P. and Axell, K., Armed conflict at the end of the Cold War, *Journal of Peace Research*, 30, 331–346, 1993; Wallensteen, P. and Sollenberg, M., The end of international war? Armed conflict 1989–1995, *Journal of Peace Research*, 33, 353–370, 1996; Petter Gleditsch, N., *et al.*, Armed conflict 1946-2001: a new dataset, *Journal of Peace Research*, 39, 615–637, 2002. Also Tilly, Ch., op. cit., Cambridge UP, Cambridge, 57ff, 2003. The concept of 'New Wars' was first used by Kaldor, M., *New and Old Wars. Organized Violence in a Global Era*, Polity Press, Cambridge, 1999.

15. van Creveld, M., *The Transformation of War*, Free Press, New York, 1991; Huntington, S., *The Clash of Civilizations and the Remaking of World Order*, Simon and Schuster, New York, 1996.

16. Horowitz, D.L., *Ethnic Groups in Conflict*, University of California Press, Berkeley, 5, 1985. In a quantitative empirical study, it has been demonstrated that the prevalence of internal war in the 1990s is mainly the result of an accumulation of protracted conflicts since the 1950s, because decolonisation gave birth to a large number of financially, bureacratically and militarily weak states. See Fearon, J.D. and Laitin, D.D., Ethnicity, insurgency and civil war, *American Political Science Review*, 97, 75–90, 2003.

17. Koonings, K. and Kruijt, D., (eds.), *Societies of Fear. The Legacy of Civil War, Violence and Terror in Latin America*, ZED Books, London and New York, 1999.

18. See Fearon, J.D. and Laitin, D.D., op. cit., 83, 2003; Collier, P. and Hoeffert, A., On economic causes of civil war, *Oxford Economic Papers*, 50, 563–568, 1998; Petter Gleditsch, N. *et al.*, op. cit., 624, 2002; Doyle M.W. and Sambanis, N., International peacekeeping: a theoretical and quantitative analysis, *American Political Science Review*, 94, 779–781 and 789, 2000.

19. See Fearon, J.D. and Laitin, D.D., op. cit., 85, 2003; Doyle M.W. and Sambanis, N., op. cit., 789, 2000; Collier and Hoeffert, op. cit., 568–569, 1998; as they have put it, 'possessing natural resources makes things worse...'. About the connection between oil and the conflict in the Sudan, see Lam Both, P., *South Sudan: Forgotten Tragedy*, Calgary UP, Calgary, 9–11, 2002; Broch-Due, V. (ed.), *Violence and Belonging. The Quest for Identity in Post-colonial Africa*, Routledge, London and New York, Chapter 7, 2005. About diamonds, see Campbell, G., *Blood Diamonds. Tracing the Deadly Path of the World Most Precious Stones*, Westview Press, Boulder, 2002.

20. This process has been described tellingly in Kaplan, R.D., *The Ends of the Earth. A Journey at the Dawn of the 21st Century*, Random House, New York, 1996.

21. Beck, U., *Risk society. Towards a New Modernity*, Sage, London, 1992.

22. Esler, G., *The United States of Anger*, Penguin Books, London, 1997.

23. See Kymlicka, W., *Politics in the Vernacular. Nationalism, Multiculturalism and Citizenship*, Oxford UP, Oxford, 2001. See also Castells, M., *The Power of Identity, Second Edition*, Blackwell, Oxford, 2004.

24. For descriptions of the religiously inspired 'madness' of people, see, for instance, Juergensmeyer, M., *Terror in the Mind of God. The Global Rise of Religious Violence*, University of California Press, Berkeley, 2000; Tibi, B., *The Challenge of Fundamentalism. Political Islam and the New World Disorder*, University of California Press, Berkeley, 2002.

25. See Kaldor, M., op. cit., 1999; Campbell, op. cit., 2002; Volkov, V., Violent entrepeneurship in post-Communist Russia, *Europe-Asia Studies*, 51, 741–754, 1999.

26. See Collins, R., On the microfoundations of macrosociology, *American Journal of Sociology*, 86, 984–1014, 1981.

27. See Collins, R., op. cit., 1981. A more precise subdivision would entail three categories — long-term developments, short-term developments and short-term events; see also Arts, W., op. cit., 1996. Another categorisation could be mechanisms, processes and episodes in McAdam, D., *et al.*, op. cit., 2001. Due to the introductory character of the book, I prefer to keep matters simple,

13

for which reason I stick to a division into two groups of mechanisms and processes, namely the long-term macro developments and the short-term micro-events.

28. Horowitz, D.L., op. cit., 1985; Kaufman, S.J., Spiraling to ethnic war, *International Security*, 21, 108–138, 1996.

Part I

MACRO AND LONG-TERM FACTORS

2

GRID CHARACTERISTICS AND GROUP BOUNDARIES

The conflicts that are currently drawing our attention have made us familiar with the various ethnic or culture-bound groups fighting each other. In Bosnia, the fight was between the Serbs, Muslims and Croats and even between mixed groups, such as the Bosnian Serbs and the Croatian Serbs. In Rwanda, there was opposition between the Hutus and the Tutsis. In Somalia, the conflicts between the traditional tribe-related clans, like the Abgals and the Murusade, constitute a background of violence, similar to Liberia, Sierra Leone and the Sudan. In the Caucasus, Chechen clans continue their struggle against the Russian army which contains troops from St Petersburg, Moscow and Siberia. Yet the Chechen capital Grozny has, for generations, been the residence of tens of thousands of ethnic Russian families, who are at their wits' end, caught in the thick of the fighting between the warring parties. They are in exactly the same tight position as the French families in the former 'department' of Algeria during the decolonisation war of 1961, or as the Dutch families in the Dutch East Indies at the time of police action in the late 1940s.

What is the background to all this? In order to sketch that background, a typology developed by British anthropologist Mary Douglas may be useful.[1] In her analysis of societies, she distinguishes two dimensions — grid and group. The grid dimension refers to the social distinctions applying to individuals and can be either strongly or poorly developed. If it is strongly developed in a society or organisation, then fixed rules and regulations, clear rights and duties, transparent classifications and unchallenged differences in status and symbols exist. All this leads to clearly defined social 'roles' on the basis of an accepted allocation of status and division of labour. The interaction between these 'role players' is regulated to a considerable extent, which means it is laid down in prescribed behaviour. Thus a recognisable and universally acceptable distinction is made between employees with paid work and self-employed people, labourers and retailers, pensioners and students, people on unemployment benefits and employed people, the healthy and the ailing, administrators and the electorate and between the various professions (e.g. regular service personnel, accountants, trained nurses). Every social role has a set of rights and duties, which everyone agrees to. A strong grid has an unchallenged social order and is objective and universal at first sight.

To get a clearer view of matters, the army is a classical example of a strong grid at the organisation level. The army has a narrowly defined hierarchy of functions, clearly subdivided into units labelled Arms and Services. The military pyramid also has a strict division of authority, which is visible, known and acceptable to everyone. Besides the armed forces, the monastery and the Roman Catholic Church in general, are also examples of organisations with a strongly developed grid. Everyone taking part in this kind of organisation or community knows their position, the rights and duties that go with it and the appropriate conduct.

However, when there is a poor grid, the differentiation of social roles and hierarchical order into social 'layers' is either limited or non-existent. In such a situation, there will be constant negotiations, quarrels and reproaches about ambitions and goals, about the rights and duties connected with the various social roles and the corresponding status. An example of this phenomenon in the Western world concerns the shifting rights and duties of men and women. Until not so long ago, women took care of the household whereas men earned a living outside the house. There was no discussion possible. This social pattern has changed in the last few decades in that women have increasingly taken up jobs outside the house. This development went hand in hand with discussions and tensions at all levels of society, from the micro level of the family, through the meso level of organisations, to the macro level of politics. Even today, it can be said that this development has not ended yet, particularly when women still do not have the same career opportunities as men, or when men are not sufficiently willing to do their bit in the household.

A strong grid can be found in societies with stable local structures. Examples were the relatively isolated, primitive or tribal communities in what is now called the Third World, although this was true only until World War II. The grid in those communities was disrupted in the post-war turbulence caused by the decolonisation processes and later, by the disappearance of the balance of power between the United States and the Soviet Union.[2] The subsequent continuous globalisation further endangered the stable grid that existed in those communities.

Generally, the better developed the grid, the less the structure of society is disputed and the more solidly it is anchored. Nowadays, this is particularly true for the established democracies in the West. That is why, in Western societies, differences between social categories (e.g. between the employed and the unemployed) are ideologically justified. That is also why there are rules in the field of education, labour, social security, taxation, environmental planning, etc. that hold good for the entire country and every social subcategory. These rules apply to all categories of people in society and as such (almost) everyone abides by them. It is so self-evident in Western societies that these rules apply to everyone, that no one really thinks this is special anymore. The making of these rules, by way of democratic procedures and maintaining them by way of an elaborate legal system, is also nearly undisputed. In Western countries, social integration is a success and a universally accepted, detailed interference by the state has penetrated almost all spheres of life. Despite the already mentioned shifting division of roles between men and women and certain tendencies towards a deregulation of government policy, the grid dimension is relatively well developed in many Western countries.[3]

Strong grid characteristics, however, cannot be found all over the world. This has consequences in terms of the possibility of new conflicts. In societies with a limited grid, there is relatively more political and social unrest, because then, there is room for competition and struggle between persons and for positions. Conversely, in societies with a strongly developed grid, there is more peace and harmony between people.[4] This also corresponds with the second distinction made by Mary Douglas.

The second dimension concerns group cohesion. This phenomenon is governed by rules that determine who belong to a group and who do not, and by the question whether there are clear or vague group boundaries. In many cases, these boundaries between groups are determined by primordial ties. They are characteristics a person already possesses at birth or which develop during the formative years. They are so-called ascriptive characteristics, attributed to humans, which they cannot (much) influence. These characteristics can be summarised as the 'four Rs' —race, religion, region (nation) and record. The first three speak for themselves, but the latter requires some clarification. 'Record' stands for a common history, shared adventures, a common culture and sometimes a shared language or dialect. Tribes are examples of groups with a common 'record', sometimes with their own racial features. Groups that rally behind a certain goal or ambition, such as political parties, clubs, societies and workers' associations also have a common 'record'.

Examples of such groups in the Netherlands, for instance, are the traditional religious denominations (Protestants and Roman Catholics); the various regional groups such as the Frisians, Zealanders and Limburgers; the indigenous Dutch population as contrasted to migrant groups from Turkey and Morocco and people from ex-colonies (Surinam, the Moluccas); people from Amsterdam versus those from Rotterdam; people living in an urban agglomeration or in the provinces, and, finally, political groups such as Liberals versus Christian Democrats and Socialist Party members. In another country, Bolivia, group distinctions refer to the indigenous people, 'Indians' consisting of some thirty tribes as well as to Afro-Bolivians with their own historical 'record' and Europeans, who are predominantly Spanish. In nations all over the globe, such groups can be distinguished, but the importance of these group distinctions varies.

An important aspect of group distinction is how much the group lays a claim on a person's life. If this is high, as in a traditional village community, then the group dimension is strong. Then, there is a clear 'us/them' perspective; one village versus another, or as in ancient Greece, one city state (Athens) versus the other (Sparta). The individual has no chance of escaping from the pressure of the group existing within their community. Moreover, there is little room for discussion in the group. Group cohesion also has an emphatic subjective side — there is a sense of oneness with the group, loyalty and a real experience of group feeling. When the group dimension is strongly developed, in other words, when there are clear group boundaries that are also experienced as such by the other members of the group, then people reject the other, the unknown. This process is intensified when various criteria for group boundaries overlap — in Scotland, Glasgow Rangers football fans are Protestants without exception, whereas the Glasgow Celtic supporters are all Roman Catholics. The same is true when religious and ethnic divisions are congruent, as in Sri Lanka between the Hindu Tamils and the Buddhist Sinhalese.[5] This effect has even greater impact when religion and place of residence coincide with each other — in Belfast, Northern Ireland, the Protestants live in areas other than those occupied by the Roman Catholics, as can be seen in the map in Figure 2.

BLACK = CATHOLIC NEIGHBOURHOODS
LIGHT = PROTESTANT NEIGHBOURHOODS

Figure 2 Distribution of Protestants and Catholics in Belfast. (Reprinted with permission from *Le Monde Diplomatique, Atlas of Globalization*, 2003)

Therefore, group feeling is not only based on religion but also on the area or neighbourhood where people live. In as far as group distinctions lead to violent conflicts (which need not necessarily be the case, as we shall see), outbursts of rage often occur, when one group organises provocative marches or demonstrations through the neighbourhood of the 'others'. This has happened frequently over the years, not only in Northern Ireland but also in India and other places in Southern Asia.[6]

A contemporary manifestation of group building, as it is developing in the United States at any rate, is the tendency of homosexuals to settle down in their own districts. By creating neighbourhoods with a homosexual baker, a homosexual general practitioner and a gay bicycle repair man, the spatial segregation of homosexuals is slowly but firmly taking shape. In the Netherlands, attempts are even being made to found retirement homes solely for elderly homosexuals. Although there are ample indications that in modern Western societies there has been a distinct decline of group building or compartmentalisation (on the basis of political or religious orientation), this example points in the opposite direction. Among citizens from former Dutch colonies (e.g. Surinamese Dutch) too, tendencies towards group building can be observed, which is illustrated by the fact that they desire to be united in political parties of their own ('Black Reveille'). The idea behind it is that the participation of Surinamese Dutchmen in the 'established' political parties provides little benefit for the group, but that this may improve if one or more of their own political parties are founded. In Bolivia, indigenous groups no longer recognise themselves in existing political parties dominated by the Europeans. That is why they are striving for political movements of their own, which is a development that seems to be occurring on a worldwide scale nowadays.[7]

When there is strong group building and, consequently, clearly delineated group boundaries, then the person who 'defects' to another group is referred to as a 'traitor', 'defector' or 'renegade'. This process is clearly shown in the motion picture '*Dances with Wolves*'. This alternative Western portrays the adventures of a white officer in the American Civil War, who chooses to live among Sioux Indians and adopts the Sioux identity in appearance, language and gestures. When he falls into the hands of his former fellow-soldiers of the Northern Army, he is called 'traitor'. But that is not all. Calling him a traitor also provides the alibi for beating him up and making him their prisoner. That is still mild treatment. In the former Yugoslavia, young men who refused to serve in the military during the war were threatened with the serious consequences their refusal would have for their parents and relatives (such as losing work and home).[8] But it can be even worse: summary executions of defectors are certainly no exception in times of conflict.

The effect of defection can also be the reverse. The defector himself may totally lose control due to an identity change. Every conflict has a few examples of that. One, for instance, is the case of a Tutsi who defected to the opposing side, the Hutus, and completely adopted the Hutu identity. To prove his loyalty to the new group, he went after the Tutsis, his former fellow-tribesmen, with increased fanaticism. Besides that, he made daily radio broadcasts which were downright inciting. Two years later, the person in question was accused of inciting genocide and for taking a personal lead in the massacre of hundreds of Tutsis. He became one of the prime suspects of the Rwandan genocide of 1994.[9]

However, the group dimension can also be weakly developed, which can be recognised by vague group boundaries and simultaneous memberships in many groups. The notion of who belongs to which group changes according to the situation. The same person can be a member of different groups, none of which puts much of a claim on that person. In many Western countries, such as the Netherlands, group distinctions do exist as we saw before, but the impact of membership on any group is relatively limited. A supporter of the Amsterdam football club Ajax, for instance, may be employed by the multinational Philips, which is the main sponsor of the competing club in another part of the country. Likewise, a Roman Catholic can attend a Protestant church service. The boundaries are not clearly drawn and there may be overlap. In general, the group dimension is less strongly developed when representatives of different groups meet each other frequently, as happens in an urban environment. This may result in 'mixed' relations, such as 'mixed' friendships and marriages. In such a situation, there is generally room for a tolerant, pragmatic attitude towards life. One is open to the unfamiliar in a social (one keeps contact with foreigners) as well as cognitive respect (one is susceptible to ideas from outside). This is also referred to as the 'strength of weak ties' as opposed to the 'weakness of strong ties', which arises when one locks oneself up in the closely-knit bastion of one's own group.[10]

Group, grid and the risk of conflict

It is obvious that tolerance for one another takes root less when there are clearly defined group boundaries between people. Tolerance can be described as granting the right to exist to something that does not belong to you or you do not really respect. Conversely, when there is more group 'blending' due to overlapping group boundaries and frequent encounters between groups, there is greater tolerance for one another. In social psychology, this is called the effect of the 'contact hypothesis'. Its validity has been demonstrated in a research based on an extensive survey held among the population of the former Yugoslavia. The survey was held only just before the violent hostilities started there.[11] The effect of a strongly developed group dimension was clearly shown in the religion of the respondents. The more religious they were, the more intolerant they were towards others. This research result corresponds with other, everyday observations about the intolerant and antagonistic attitude of religious fundamentalists.[12] The opposite effect was clearly revealed in a number of other findings. People of mixed marriages (e.g. between a Serb woman and a Croat male and between a Muslim woman and a Serb male) and people living in areas where the population was highly mixed (usually urban areas such as Sarajevo and Banja Luka), turned out to be more tolerant.

Grid plays a particularly important role in the violence and rage that group distinctions may bring about. It should be noted that ethnic or religious group distinctions, as such, do not cause violent conflicts. This has been demonstrated unequivocally in a number of quantitative studies.[13] Only in connection with the grid dimension, group diversity in societies may promote rage and fury. When the grid is relatively weakly developed and group boundaries are very clear, then there is a higher chance of intolerance and tensions. This can be seen in the bottom-right square in Figure 3.

There are also weakly developed or undeveloped institutional arrangements within society (e.g. in the field of conscription, law enforcement, jurisdiction, taxation or education), which cut straight through the group distinctions and diminish the effects of group dynamics. A weak grid implies

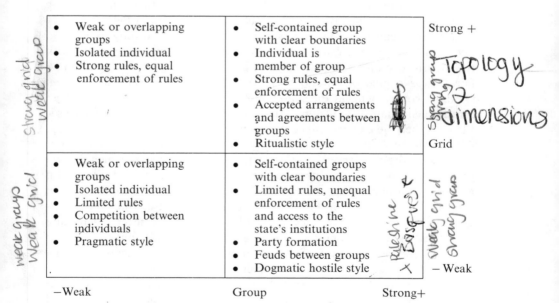

Figure 3 Violence and conflict in the group–grid model. Source: Boon, L., *De list der wetenschap (The Ruse of Science)*, Ambo, Baarn, especially pages 159 and 167, 1983.

that there are no rights and duties that apply equally to every member of society. This means that the effect of the weakly developed grid is too minimal to compensate for the strong group effect. An example is a weak or biased system of jurisdiction leading to some groups of people systematically being prosecuted and punished more frequently and severely than others.

Another example to illustrate this mechanism is the so-called civil service issue. This term refers to the phenomenon of distribution of civil service jobs (army and police included) that takes place on the basis of division into groups and group relations, and not on the basis of objective criteria such as assessing a person's professional adequacy for the job. Every ethnically divided society, from a country like Belgium to countries on the African continent, has its own civil service issue. However, there may be differences in the way it is dealt with. When there is a strong grid (the square in the top right-hand corner), the civil service issue is approached from a ritualistic angle, which means that it is in line with existing customs and in accordance with the rules and arrangements agreed to by all parties. These are often agreements or rules that serve to protect minorities. These rules are applied to make sure that all groups in society can benefit from the proportional distribution of positions in the army, police, the judiciary and the civil service.

This is, for example, the case in Belgium, where positions and posts are neatly and proportionally distributed among each group in Belgian society (Walloons, Flemish and German speaking Belgians), according to existing, poignantly accurate arrangements. These arrangements came along with the (quasi-)federalisation that Belgium introduced in the 1980s, granting a fairly large degree of autonomy to the Walloon, Flemish and German speaking governments at the sub-national level. At the national level, these arrangements imply, for instance, that when the Director of Fiscal Policies is Flemish, then the Deputy will be Walloon. But then, the Director of Foreign Affairs will be Walloon and the Deputy, Flemish. These agreements are not exclusive to the civil services, but apply to all circumstances in which the two groups have to work together, as in the Belgian Army. At the Royal Military School in Brussels, lectures are given both in Flemish and in French. The Belgian Air Force has one air force base where French is spoken and another where they speak Flemish. There is never a departure from these agreements and regulations, even when it is obvious to everyone that they are basically inefficient and senseless. These agreements have only been made to maintain harmony between the parties. The customs are clear to everyone, which indicates that the civil service issue has been arranged in a manner acceptable to everybody. There are enough checks and balances, rules and agreements, in short, enough institutions, to preserve the precarious balance between the groups.[14] A comparable example is the European Union, with its interpreters and translators for each of the languages of its member states. Strictly speaking, this phenomenon is inefficient and expensive, but it means that all the countries, even the smallest, are accepted for what they are. In this way, the need for everybody to adapt, presumably with very great reluctance, to the most widely spoken language, in this case German, can be avoided.

In a weak grid (the bottom-right square in Figure 3), functions in political and government office are divided on the basis of the power relations existing between rival groups. Then, the stronger group dominates the weaker and group dynamics dominate the grid. In the former Yugoslavia, this was obviously the case. In Croatia and Bosnia, the Serbs were strongly represented in the Communist Party, the police, public services and state enterprises, which was the result of Tito's deliberate and authoritarian divide-and-rule policy. This Serbian over-representation in the government machinery was the greatest thorn in the side of the Croatian Party, which was seeking independence. As soon as the Croatian Party saw its way clear, short shrift was made of this practice.[15] In areas where the Serbs retained their dominant position, as in Bosnian Serbia, all Muslims and Croats whose work gave them access to important information were dismissed when the tension increased. They became unemployed overnight without being entitled to any unemployment benefit and were sometimes evicted from their houses.[16] However, such occurrences certainly do not make the situation in the former Yugoslavia unique.

This is a worldwide phenomenon. Malaysia is a society with large ethnic minorities (20% Chinese and 10% Indian), where employment in the public services, the army and the police is almost exclusively reserved for 'real' Malays. In the Sudan, Islamic law dictates that non-believers are not eligible for the highest political posts in Khartoum.[17] In Rwanda, Tutsis have had a dominant position in society and the civil service, in particular since colonial times (1930s). This 'Tutsification' of public administration has created and worsened tensions between the Hutus and the Tutsis, ultimately leading to the slaughter of 800,000 Tutsis in 1994.[18] The same problem also still exists in Northern Ireland, where 'time and again, it is the civil service issue that highlights grievances'. It is interesting to know in this respect that this phenomenon once occurred in the Netherlands too. In the prosperous sixteenth and seventeenth centuries, only adherents to the Dutch Reformed faith could hold government office. The civil service issue is a clear form of what is elsewhere referred to as 'ethnic nepotism', i.e. favouring the members of one's own group, and this has unmistakably been proved to be a source of irritation and conflict.[19]

With respect to the police and the armed forces, the civil service issue is so much more important, because selectively composed uniformed organisations tend to act in a biased manner when they are expected to intervene in riots, upheaval and violent conflict. Not intervening, selectively taking drastic action, or even participating in the chase of targeted groups has often aggravated the situation considerably. Such selective behaviour has often played an exacerbating role in ethnic riots in Southern Asia (India, Pakistan). For example, in ethnic rivalries between Hindus and Muslims in Bombay in the 1990s, the police forces, with a vast majority of non-Muslims, actively participated in indiscriminate shooting, the larger number of their victims being Muslims.[20] As recent as 2003, the Bolivian armed forces, with virtually only officers of Spanish descent in their ranks, controlled protest demonstrations of indigenous people in the streets of La Paz by killing some 100 of them. It is highly unlikely that they would have resolved the problems in this manner if the protesters had been predominantly of Spanish or generally European origin.[21]

Generally, when there are strong group dynamics and weak grid characteristics, a dogmatic, conflicting orientation on man, society and life prevails. In these kinds of societies, the different groups behave as closed enclaves, which resist the outside world. Then, a kind of 'monster-thinking' pervades these enclaves — there is one single exclusive world-view and everything else (all other groups and ideologies) are looked upon as a 'monster' or a 'demon' that has to be exorcised. If there is no other way, then force must be used to do it.

On the other hand, social integration, manifesting itself in a highly developed grid (hence, from the bottom-right square to the square in the top-right), subdues the inclination of groups of people living side by side to start a conflict. As in the Belgian example, there is often a ritualistic approach to problems and potential conflicts. Whenever there is the threat of conflict, it is possible to fall back on agreements, rules and conventions to relieve group tensions. Less group dynamics or 'depillarisation' (from the bottom-right square to the bottom-left one) reduces the inclination among groups to start a conflict. Then, society consists more of individuals continuously competing with each other in the social and economic sphere. This kind of depillarised society is, above all, characterised by a tolerant, pragmatic lifestyle.

It is not surprising, therefore, that in modern Western European societies, very little ethnic or communal violence remains. On the one hand, this has to do with depillarisation, the fading of group distinctions, concurrent with the modernisation of those societies. In the Netherlands, for instance, the difference between Roman Catholics and Protestants was still a serious matter in the 1950s, which certainly, at neighbourhood level, could give rise to serious and violent confrontations among youth. Nowadays, in the Netherlands, people often cannot tell another person's religious persuasion, if any. The 'big stories' in religion and politics (the 'Socialists'!) have lost much of their significance over the past few decades, as post-modernism has taught us. Religion and politics are not of such great importance anymore.[22] However, there may be cause for some concern about the periodic attacks on mosques in the Netherlands and in other Western European countries, such as Belgium, France and the UK There certainly is also some anxiety when Moroccan-Dutch youth are in the news because of their violent approach (in the shape of physical violence, abuse, etc.) towards members of the Jewish community.[23]

There undoubtedly are culture- and language-bound groups still to be found in Western societies (in fact, to an increasing extent since the arrival of ethnic 'newcomers'), but a strong grid takes the edge off its negative aspects. In this respect, it suffices to consider countries like Switzerland and Belgium, as was previously indicated. It must be noted, however, that these modern, but also 'ethnically divided', Western societies not only show a relatively strong grid but also weaker group dynamics than in the familiar conflict areas such as the former Yugoslavia and various African countries. Depillarisation and individualisation have also strongly affected these 'ethnically divided', but modern Western countries. This has to do with their national culture, a subject that will be discussed at a later stage. In sum, a strong grid, along with weak group dynamics, limits the inclination within societies to start a conflict.[24]

A final remark will conclude this. When both group dynamics and grid are relatively weak (the bottom-left square), there is a tolerant, pragmatic lifestyle among competing individuals. However, this tolerance may lead to another problem, namely powerlessness and indifference. Then, the fact that somebody is mugged in the street, or a bike is stolen, a woman is harassed or employees are sacked, is not interesting anymore and an attitude of 'tough luck' or 'your problem, not mine' prevails. Nobody stands up for another person anymore, although there may be need for it. There is too little commitment or social cohesion between people. This disposition explains much of the criminal behaviour and feelings of uncertainty and insecurity existing in modern societies. Some consider this the core problem of modern Western societies. However distressing these problems may be, they are quite remote from the violent intranational conflicts that are the central issue of this study. The inclination to start conflicts of this kind is, once again, primarily influenced by strong group dynamics in combination with weak grid.

However, inclination is not the same as the actual outbreak of conflicts. It takes a bit more than that; amongst other things, the factors described in the next chapter.

Notes

1. See Douglas, M., *Natural Symbols. Explorations in Cosmology*, Barrie & Rockliffe, London, 54–64, 1970. A more transparent explanation of the theory (published by Douglas, M. in 1973) can be found in Collins, R., *Four Sociological Traditions. Selected Readings*, Oxford University Press, Oxford, 271–280, 1994. Applications of this model can be found in Boon, L., *De list der*

wetenschap (The Ruse of Science), Ambo, Baarn, especially Chapters 6 and 7, 1983, as well as in Schuyt, K., *Arbeidstijdsverkorting en maatschappelijke orde* (Working time reduction and societal order), von Grumbkow, J. and Godschalk, J.J. (eds.), *Sociale aspecten van arbeidstijdverkorting (Social Aspects of Working Time Reduction)*, Swets en Zeitlinger, Lisse, 165–174, 1984. The application and interpretation of this model is the author's. An application of this theory on the origins and development of terrorist violence can be found in Douglas, M. and Mars, G., Terrorism: a positive feedback game, *Human Relations*, 56, 763–786, 2003.

2. Douglas, M., 1973 in Collins, R., op. cit., 276, 1994.

3. For example, de Swaan, A., *In Care of the State. Health Care, Education and Welfare in Europe and the U.S.A in the Modern Era*, Polity, Cambridge, 1988.

4. Douglas, M., 1973 in Collins, R., op. cit., 1994; Boon, L., op. cit., 1983.

5. Manor, J., The failure of political integration, *Journal of Commonwealth and Comparative Politics*, 17, 21–46, 1989; see also; Tambiah, S.J., op. cit., 39, 1996.

6. Tambiah, S.J., op. cit., 1996.

7. Kymlicka, W., op. cit., 2001.

8. Faber, M., *Novi Dani, nieuwe dagen. Oorlog en biografie in Banja Luka, Bosnië-Herzegovina (Novi Dani, New Days. War and Biography in Banja Luka, Bosnia Hercegovina)*, Aksant, Amsterdam, 103, 2001.

9. Anonymous article, *Hij heeft mijn man en 26 buren gedood* (He has killed my husband and 26 neighbours). *Guardian/Volkskrant*, 17 January 1997, p.4.

10. See Granovetter, M., The strength of weak ties, *American Journal of Sociology*, 78, 1360–1380, 1973.

11. Hodson, R., Sekulic, D. and Massey, G., National tolerance in the former Yugoslavia, *American Journal of Sociology*, 99, 1534–1558, 1994; Faber, M., op. cit., 126, 2001.

12. Roberts, R., Interpretations of resurgent religion, *Theory, Culture and Society*, 13, 129–138, especially page 131, 1996; Tibi, B., op. cit., 2002.

13. Fearon, J.D. and Laitin, D.D., op. cit., 2003; Collier, P. and Hoeffert, A., op. cit., 1998; Doyle, M.W. and Sambanis, N., op. cit., 789, 2000.

14. Lake, D.A. and Rotchild, D., Containing fear. The origins and management of ethnic conflict, *International Security*, 49, 1996; about Belgium, see Hooghe, L., Belgium. From regionalism to federalism, in Coakly, J. (ed.), *The Territorial Management of Ethnic Conflict* (2nd and rev. edn), Frank Cass, London, 73–98, 2002.

15. Glenny, M., op. cit., 13, 1993; Bax, M., *Medjugorje: Religion, Politics, and Violence in Rural Bosnia*, VU University Press, Amsterdam 1995. For a more general description of the 'civil service issue' in ethnically divided states, see Horowitz, D.L., op. cit., 224–226, 1985.

16. Faber, M., op. cit., 60–61, 2001.

17. Information obtained from Luciëlla Boeddha, who adds that she might have been biased during her stay in Malaysia because of her continuous interaction with Chinese Malaysians; apparently the whole issue still plays a role in the country. About Sudan, see Scroggins, D., op. cit., 2002.

18. de Temmerman, E., op. cit., 247–261, 1994.

19. Horowitz, D.L., op. cit., 238, 1985. About ethnic nepotism as a source of conflicts, see Vanhanen, T., Domestic ethnic conflict and ethnic nepotism: a comparative analysis, *Journal of Peace Research*, 36, 55–73, 1999. About the civil service issue in the Netherlands in the 16th and 17th centuries, see Lammers, C.J., *Nederland als bezettende mogendheid* 1648–2001 (The Netherlands as an Occupying Power), KNAW, Amsterdam, 2003.

20. Tambiah, S.J., op. cit., pages 254, 132 and 176, 1996.

21. The killing of some 100 protesting members of indigenous groups in the streets of La Paz caused the resignation of the Bolivian government and subsequently led to drastic attempts to change the diversity climate within the armed forces.

22. For example, Bauman, Z., *Intimations of Postmodernity*, Routledge, London, 1992.

23. Anonymous article, *Joden voelen zich ontheemd in hun eigen Mokum* (Jews feel estranged in their own Amsterdam), *Volkskrant*, 1 November 2003. Similar accounts are regularly recorded in major cities in France.

24. Horowitz, D.L., op. cit., 19, 1985.

3

WANING GOVERNMENT, DEMOCRATIC DEFICIT AND STRATEGIC CONSTELLATION

The current 'ordinary people' conflicts have developed against the background of the end of an era, the *Pax Atomica*. The world is no longer dominated by the balance of power that kept in check the Eastern and the Western blocks, as well as the smaller players wedged in between. Now, the world has turned multi-centric, creating more space for the ambitions of the lower administrative and social echelons, such as the smaller countries, regions or ethnic and cultural population groups. Present day conflicts have developed against this background, usually as a result of the breakdown of a national centre of power. This has clearly been the case in the former Yugoslavia, where Tito's death signalled the disintegration of the state and the start of all the conflicts and the violence that went together.[1] The disturbances in Somalia began after the fall of the dictator Siad Barre. Rwanda saw the beginning of unrest on 6 April 1994 after an attack on a government airplane, which killed the Presidents of both Burundi and Rwanda. Other African conflicts as well as skirmishes in the former Soviet Union had comparable causes.

This, as such, is a familiar fact that can be explored further from a sociological angle. An important starting point in sociology is that many occurrences are the unintentional result of intentional, therefore purposeful actions of (groups of) humans.[2] This happens when humans are part of networks of mutual dependencies, which branch off the more a society modernises. Production processes and business transactions extending increasingly further internationally, may serve as an example here.

The more complex these networks or figurations become, the more the share of unintentional consequences in human intercourse grows. They are called strategic constellations, in which 'people are responding to an environment that consists of other people responding to their environment, which consists of people responding to an environment of people's responses'.[3] In such a strategic constellation, nobody can really calculate the extent and effects of their actions. But more important is that in increasingly complex networks nobody seems to be able to really bring about the intended effects. As figurations become more complex and

30

expand, nobody can operate without relying on others. Nobody, not even a single political centre, will then be so dominant as to be able to impose its will upon other parties. The more the 'game' between people (groups, nations) has more players, dimensions and rules to play by, the less the predictability and the potential to bend the outcome to one's own preferences.

This insight is important for the explanation of the origin of present day conflicts. Conflicts occur where, until quite recently, absolute power centres were able to control large areas. As societal communities modernise and dependency networks expand and thicken (for example, by the internationalisation of economic transactions and the intensification of international contacts by way of increasingly modern communication media), the existence of centres of absolute power is becoming less possible.

World history reveals that all great empires meet their downfall, mostly caused by their own success. There are at least two reasons for that. First, because of their continuous success, they have the tendency to continue to expand to such a high level that eventually all control is lost. This could be referred to as geopolitical expansion or imperial over-stretching. It seems a pendant of the so-called Peter Principle, as it is known in organisational science — because of their excellent achievements, human beings make frequent promotions until they reach a position in which they turn out to be incompetent. Besides that, the creation of an empire usually leads to economic growth. Up and down the empire that process leads to expectations which, at a certain point, cannot be fulfilled anymore. As a consequence, both the economic and military manageability decline, in which case the legitimacy, or rather the acceptance, of the central power decreases.[4]

This pattern is characteristic of the decay of quite a number of world empires, examples of which are the Roman Empire, Byzantium, the Ottoman Empire and the seventeenth century Spanish Empire. In the modernising world, with its open world economy and international data flows, the above mentioned mechanisms of over-expansion and loss of controllability and legitimacy are much more strongly felt. This process clearly came to light in the decolonisation era. It proved impossible not only for small countries, such as the Netherlands and Portugal, but also larger countries such as England and France, to manage and control large overseas areas permanently. While the colonisation process expanded enormously at the beginning of the nineteenth century as a result of the Industrial Revolution, the industrialisation process in turn marked the process of decolonisation. The latter process led to the first wave of liberation and independence of countries.

The modern world, with the internationalisation of economic transactions in the latter part of the twentieth century, has proved that it is even more inevitable that large-scale, centralised, absolute power should make way for the autonomy of, and competition between, the more small-scale levels of administration. Although currently considered supreme, even the United States is experiencing the limitations of its military power in Iraq and has great worries about its trade deficit with countries like Japan and, more recently, China. Apparently the United States senses that its military and economic might are swiftly waning.

When control by a single central power bloc becomes impossible, often there is the problem of a power vacuum that cannot be filled in an adequate and 'civilised' way. The situation often arises that the governmental unit (the nation) that emerges in this power vacuum is rather 'artificial'. The 'unnatural' character of many nations may manifest itself in two ways. Colonial powers and communist empire builders often created nations in which population groups, which used to live scattered or independently in a smaller sector, were put together. On the other hand, they recurrently created borders that cut across population groups. Western colonialism and communist imperialism have frequently created administrative scales without taking into account the original small-scale local and regional structures.[5]

The carelessness with which European nations divided Africa at the end of the nineteenth and beginning of the twentieth centuries is now, in retrospect, absolutely baffling. In the chanceries of England, France and Germany, national boundaries were drawn on the map of Africa on the basis of the internal power considerations in Europe. There was no knowledge of the precise geographical circumstances (mountains, rivers) on site, let alone any understanding of, or consideration for, the social and political circumstances of the indigenous population. In less than half a century, this boundary-making turned the fluid networks of communities into fixed societies that were 'essentialised and enumerated' and where special passports were issued to prevent 'trespassing' across national, and even district boundaries.[6] This situation also occurred in the Middle and Far East, as well as in the former Soviet Union and the former Yugoslavia. In all these regions, the central or colonial rulers created boundaries in the course of time, which did and still does not do justice to the original social, ethnic and political situation in the respective areas. The history of the former Soviet Union is especially telling in this respect. During the Stalin era, large populations groups were deported from their homelands. This deportation policy had an especially pervasive impact on the southern flank of the state. In the 1940s and 1950s, Chechens and Ingush, population groups with their own language and religion (Islam), were deported in large numbers, hence making room for Russians. This injustice dating from this period led to the 'rehabilitation and resettlement of repressed peoples' in the following decades, the late 1950s till the 1990s. In turn, these rehabilitation policies created new injustice because, as a consequence, the borders, the administrative status as well as the demographic composition of territories were changed. The impact of this could be seen in very concrete incidents. In a number of cases, especially in Chechnya, returning people claimed their houses that for decades had been occupied by others, mostly ethnic Russians. In quite a few instances, this happened under threat of deadly violence. Clearly, this has contributed to the development of mutual suspicion and strife between the population groups.[7]

Thus, decisions taken in the past provide the reason why national frontiers may cut straight through ethnic populations or why populations that formerly had nothing to do with each other were put together. Albanians, a population group that differs from virtually everybody else in the Balkans in terms of language and religion, live in Albania — the mother country — but they are also found in Kosovo and Macedonia (parts of the former Yugoslavia), as well as in Greece and Bulgaria. Particularly in Kosovo, this has led to large-scale and bloody conflicts, which necessitated massive military intervention. In Macedonia, such a conflict could only just be avoided because the international community took preventive military action. In Greece and Bulgaria, there is still popular apprehension about the creation of a greater Albanian Empire, stretching from the Adriatic to the Black Sea. In general, nation states feel uncomfortable when population groups, expanding across borders, strive for autonomy within their own state. They fear this might lead to secession and the formation of a new state together with kindred people in the neighbouring state(s). Due to these anxieties, nation states tend to fiercely suppress such emancipation movements. A clear example has been Turkey's policy towards the Kurds over the last few decades, because the Kurds live in large numbers not only in Turkey but also in neighbouring Iraq, hence potentially threatening the integrity of Turkey as a nation state. For Iraq, similar considerations have always applied. Conversely, if nationstates feel that their future as a nation state is not, or no longer threatened, they will be more inclined to recognise the claims of such population groups (with respect to the use of language, culture, religion and the like).[8]

As mentioned, the past has also created situations in which very different population groups live together in one nation state. In the Congo, the inheritance of Belgian colonialism in Africa, several population groups live in such discord with each other that some believe that only the establishment of new national boundaries can make the problems disappear. Not only would that solve the interior problems in the Congo, but also in Rwanda and elsewhere in Central Africa. There should, in fact, be a new Treaty of Berlin to review the colonial boundaries determined by the European Powers at the Treaty conference held in Berlin (1884–1885). Then, according to some, it would be possible to put an end to many conflicts in the area.[9]

The artificiality of many states rapidly becomes clear, especially when there is a power vacuum. All the more when it is realised that under previous rulers generally no culture that was favourable to the formation of democratic and legitimate groups or parties could develop. This is what is called the democratic deficit. To use the terms of the foregoing chapter — where no widely accepted social order has taken root, and where there is no rule of law, and consequently where no firm grid has developed, the basic conditions for harmony and mutual trust are missing in the event of a power vacuum. Then, only political anarchy will follow. After all, 'reciprocal trust can be induced by institutions'.[10] Institutions are rights and rules that take all parties into consideration and protect minorities; institutions are also administrative principles and, in general, arrangements and checks and balances between parties in a society. When no adequate efforts have ever been made to establish such institutions, reciprocal trust will be a long time coming.

In areas with a dictatorial and colonial past, the development of a Western democracy is usually a strenuous matter. The democratic form of government based on elections is often rejected as being too 'Western' and incompatible with native culture. Belgian journalist Els de Temmerman gave the following description: 'All too often I have seen how African leaders, in an effort to cling to power, bent democracy to chaos, how they interpreted multi-party systems in terms of ethnic division and started to abuse the freedom of speech, demanded by the West, in inciting hate campaigns.' Similar observations have regularly been recorded in many places in southern Asia.[11]

These unintended consequences of Western democracy are understandable in themselves. When voting behaviour is completely linked to group membership, the numerical relations between groups determine election results. Imagine in a country there is group A, consisting of 60% of its inhabitants and group B, consisting of 40%. If voting behaviour is totally determined by these group divisions, then group B will never be in power, not even in coalition governments. Cynically enough, fully in accordance with the norms of modern Western democracy, group A has attained 'traditional' absolute power so that it should not be worried about the others. The result is that a large minority of the population (40%) could be systematically neglected, denigrated, bullied (and denied employment and proper housing, among other things). The minority is left with only one resort — violence.

In Western European countries, including the countries with ethnic or cultural groups like Belgium and Switzerland, voting behaviour and group membership are not totally in line. This has to do with the fact that in these countries, group activity does not take place exclusively according to a single dimension. In Belgium and Switzerland, at least three criteria decide voting behaviour and the formation of political parties — language of course (the traditional dividing line in these countries), also social-economic class, and religion.[12] This has to do with the lesser degree of (unambiguous) group dynamics in these countries, which in turn is connected with a more strongly developed individualism in the more modern countries. This will be discussed in the chapter on violence and national culture.

A possible consequence may be that there will be constantly changing coalition governments in Western countries. This implies that every party can have a taste of power every once in a while. It is even more important that the person in power today always has to take the other parties into consideration because they may be the rulers or the coalition partners in the next government. Especially in African countries, but also in Bosnia after the Dayton Accords, the situation is entirely different. In the first elections after Dayton (July 1996), held in the Bosnian town of Mostar, the voting results were totally in accordance with the ethnic division of the town. That was quite a blow to post-Dayton optimism.[13] This situation has not changed since. In Iraq the division between Kurds, Sunnis and Shiites fully reflects the results of the elections. This certainly is a factor in the ongoing upheaval in the country, because the Sunni minority does not feel represented in the democratic decision making process and, hence, uses violence to make itself heard.

In Africa, this pattern of voting along ethnic lines is even more pronounced. It is therefore not surprising that in Africa, experiments with alternative democratic forms of government are done in places where the Western model of democracy has led to serious conflicts and hundreds of thousands of deaths, as was the case in Uganda. Governments of national unity, without the machinations of political parties, seem to be doing better than the 'normal', democratically chosen governments based on the Western model. Strictly speaking, this is no different from a certain return to earlier, more authoritarian forms of government. In many cases, such a solution seems like a continuation of the ruling power.[14]

All in all, nowadays, the idea that introducing democracy in non-Western countries is a guarantee for success is being questioned. There are enough indications that the introduction of democracy based on a Western model may lead to serious problems and conflicts in countries without a democratic tradition and with a very unequal distribution of wealth (as is the case in many developing countries). It is pointed out in this respect that the Western world needed dozens, if not hundreds, of years to learn how to make the democratic system work. It is only seventy years ago that the democratic Weimar Republic in Germany led to the rise of Hitler, Nazi dictatorship and the killing of millions of Jewish citizens. Besides, there is an important connection with economic development and differences in poverty. When a democracy does not keep pace with economic development and the just distribution of incomes, then it leads to more problems rather than to solutions. Harvard scholar Amy Chua points out that in many countries across the world certain ethnic minorities are extremely rich and elitist (for example, the whites in Zimbabwe and the Chinese in the Philippines and Indonesia). The democratically chosen majority, consisting of other, poorer groups, punishes the minorities for their richness. Being punished can actually also mean becoming victims of ethnic violence. Some authors therefore emphatically argue that the introduction of democracy in developing countries should be done cautiously and only in connection with economic development and reform.[15]

This caution is all the more important because there is also another problem attached to the introduction of democracy in developing countries. It refers to the observation that, despite democratic arrangements, there may still be a wide gap between political parties and parts of the population. The ethnic violence that has occurred in Sri Lanka since 1983 is at least partly due to the fact that the government was not fully linked to the governed. Especially the rural areas and the smaller cities saw the exclusion of their Tamil voters from the electoral rolls and Tamil parties and politicians from positions of influence within the political system. In this situation, the Tamils did not see any other way to have their voices heard than to take up arms.[16] Since 2000, Indians from Bolivia and Peru have occasionally resorted to violence because they do not feel existing political parties take their claims and grievances seriously whereas, at the same time, they do not find themselves capable of founding their own political parties.[17]

However, the decline of a centre of power, the presence of an artificially large administrative scale level and the absence of a democratic culture are not sufficient conditions in themselves for the outbreak of violent conflicts. For this to happen, a fourth factor is required, which relates to the strategic constellation of the groups. An important factor in this respect is the existence of minimal power differences between the groups. In general, more violence is used between peers than between a superior and a subordinate group or party.[18] Both must also possess enough critical mass to be able to produce force, which means that groups must be concentrated geographically and not be dispersed over an entire country. Without geographical concentration there cannot be critical mass. Besides that, there is the contrast between the centre of power and the periphery, the areas that lie at considerable distance from the centre of power. Population groups in peripheral areas are often inclined to settle their conflicts with the central government or other groups in a violent manner. This is perfectly understandable, knowing that in peripheral areas, the process of state building and creating national cultural uniformity (by means of education, the imposition of one single language, etc.) is usually the least successful, or, in any case, realised the last. Understandably, these are the areas where dialects and other variants of the principal native language continue to be spoken.[19] In peripheral areas, the legitimacy of a central government will be less than in the rest of the nation. That is why population groups in such areas (Corsica, the Basque province, Chechnya, northern Sri Lanka, the southern Sudan) are relatively rapidly inclined to strive for administrative autonomy and, if necessary, take up arms to achieve it. The smaller the power differences in these conflicts, the larger and longer lasting the hostilities and acts of violence are between the rival groups. This fact, with respect to the strategic constellation of rival groups, is also known from research into the course of large-scale, international wars.[20]

Sex ratios and deficit of peace . . . ?

Another strategic factor in a country is the distribution of men, especially young men, and women. In a number of Asian states, like Afghanistan, Bangladesh, China, India, Nepal, Pakistan and Taiwan, men clearly outnumber women. This is due to a variety of reasons resulting from gender inequality; even the killing of female babies. The result of this lack of balance between the sexes is that a number of young men have relatively low chances of getting married; this will happen especially to lower-educated, low-income males. This is the profile of people — young, unmarried, low-status males — who are likely to commit violence to solve their problems and grievances. In countries with unbalanced sex ratios, bachelor-subcultures may develop, having an aggravating effect on intranational violence and strife. These men are also more likely to fall for fundamentalist ideologies (Chapter 8) that may lead them to resort to violence and terrorism. In Afghanistan, for example, the oppressing Taliban-movement consisted(s) of young men only.

However, this phenomenon only occurs in Asia, and hence cannot explain violence all over the world. In Rwanda, for instance, the sex ratio in 1994 was normal. That must be the reason why, in a large quantitative study, the impact of the proportion of young males did not produce a significant effect on the occurrence of civil wars and insurgencies.[21]

Fights between two boxers who are each other's match last longer and are meaner than fights in which one boxer is much stronger than the other. This pugilistic comparison is relevant because in ethnic conflicts there is usually the tendency to polarise between two groups. In a conflict between two or more groups there will always be two groups left because third parties are pressured to align with one of the other two groups. This makes the comparison between them, and therefore the conflict as such, easier to survey.[22] The comparison can again be drawn with the dynamics of international conflicts, in that both parties may be confronted with a security dilemma, an arms race. When there is a balance of power, everything will be done to preserve it, even if that entails the systematic extension of the means of violence. Gradually, both sides increasingly invest in danger and insecurity.[23]

The significance of minimal power differences explains a seeming contrast, a paradox, in the former Yugoslavia. A large-scale sociological study in the former Yugoslavia claimed that in ethnically heterogeneous areas with various groups of equal size, there was a comparatively high degree of tolerance. At the same time, exactly in these areas (Bosnia, Croatia), conflicts were battled out with more bitter tenacity than in almost homogeneous parts like Serbia and Slovenia. In these latter areas, the lack of tolerance towards one another may have been much greater, but the fact that one group was clearly dominant made long lasting armed conflicts unlikely.[24] In other words, intolerance and an inclination to start a conflict are not all-decisive conditions for the actual outbreak and pursuit of violent action. The strategic power constellation on the spot is at least as important.

Generally, the former Yugoslavia offers a good illustration of the process described above. The more internationally the economy developed, the more the economic limitations of the communist system became evident. Besides, due to the influence of the means of mass communication and increased mobility (tourism in Croatia!), these limitations could no longer be kept hidden from the public at large. It was not so much Tito's death that has been instrumental in the outbreak of violence in the former Yugoslavia, it was more the apparent impossibility that somebody else (or a single party) would take over government and rule the country in the same dictatorial fashion. A multitude of factions and groups then fought over the spoils, that is to say, over the lost power or the power that was there for the taking. This happened in those areas where the composition of the population was relatively highly mixed. These conflicts could not be solved in a democratic manner because the people were not used to democracy; the authoritarian Tito regime had never bothered to foster something like a democratic culture.[25]

The downfall of the former Soviet Union happened in a more or less comparable manner. In 1986, Randall Collins published a sociological theory which predicted the demise of the Soviet Empire and, at the same time, the rise of numerous ethnic, separatist movements. He had already publicly voiced this prediction in a number of addresses and contributions to conferences in the early 1980s. It was, however, not until 1986 that he saw his argument published! His theory is about the rise and fall of states on the basis of their position in relation to other powers. In fact, this is all about the influence that strategic, geo-political (power) constellations have on the origin of conflicts. His thesis was that Russia had expanded so much in the course of centuries that it no longer lay as a 'marchland' in an open space, but found itself hemmed in as a kind of 'in-between state' with rivals on both sides. By expanding so much, the Soviet Union had over-stretched itself and the country had become weak internally. It experienced the fragility of large size — the larger a nation, the more likely that internal strife and violence will occur.[26] It is clear that this development took place in a worldwide process of intensification of economic relations and advancement in the means of communication, so that the underachieving and failing government became increasingly manifest. The centre of power fell and a democratic culture emerged, where parties or (ethnic) groups struggled for power and disturbances broke out. Seldom has a sociological prediction come true so quickly and so accurately. The ongoing unrest on the peripheral southern border of the former Soviet Union (Chechnya, Tajikistan) bears witness to that.[27]

Notes

1. See for instance, Enzensberger, H., op. cit., 1994; Burk, J., Thinking through the end of the Cold War, in Burk, J. (ed.), *The Military in New Times. Adapting Armed Forces to a Turbulent World*, Westview Press, Boulder, 1–24, 1994. With respect to the situation in the former Yugoslavia, see West, R., *Tito and the Rise and Fall of Yugoslavia*, Sinclair–Stevenson, London, 1994; Glenny, M., op. cit., 1993.

2. The idea of the unintended consequences has been developed by Robert Merton in his attempt to understand the phenomenon of the so-called 'self-fulfilling prophecy'. This idea has been elaborated in a specific way by Norbert Elias. For an excellent account, see Mennell, S., *Norbert Elias. An Introduction*, Blackwell, Oxford, 258ff, 1992.

3. Th. Schelling, *Micromotives and Macrobehavior*, Norton, New York, 1978. See also Masuch, M., Vicious circles, *Administrative Science Quarterly*, 30, 14–33, 1985.

4. For instance, Cipolla, C.M. (ed.), *The Economic Decline of Empires*, Methuen, London, 1970. Also, see Arts, W., op. cit., 18–25, 1996.

5. Horowitz, D.L., op. cit., 75–76, 1985.

6. See for example, Wesseling, H.L., *Verdeel en heers. De deling van Afrika 1880–1914 (Divide and Rule. The Division of Africa 1880–1914)*, Bert Bakker, Amsterdam, 447–461, 1992; see also Broch-Due, V. (ed.), op. cit., 8, 2005.

7. Tishkov, op. cit., 578ff, 1999. See also: Tishkov, op. cit., Chapter 3 ('contradictory modernization'), 2004.

8. Kymlicka, W., op. cit., 2001.

9. Joris, L., op. cit., 264, 2001.

10. Lake, D.A. and Rothchild, D., op. cit., 49, 1996.

11. de Temmerman, E., op. cit., 40, 1994; about Southern Asia, see Tambiah, S.J., op. Cit., 224ff, 1996.

12. Horowitz, D.L., op. cit., 83–87 and 19, 1985.

13. Anonymous, *Mostar stemt langs etnische lijnen* (Mostar votes along ethnic lines), *Volkskrant*, 3 July 1996.

14. Kuitenbrouwer, M., *Geen-partijendemocratie in Uganda* (No-party democracy in Uganda), *Intermediair*, 31, 7–9, 7 April 1995. A more recent account is Vreeken, R., *Uganda op een driesprong: geen, één of veel partijen* (Uganda at a road fork: none, one or many parties), *Volkskrant*, 10 March 2003. For a description of other than Western forms of democracy, see Sen, A., Why democratization is not the same as Westernization, *The New Republic*, 6 October 2003.

15. Chua, A., *World on Fire. How Exporting Free Market Democracy Breeds Ethnic Hatred and Global Instability*, Doubleday, New York, 2003. See also Zakaria, F.,

The Future of Freedom. Illiberal Democracy at Home and Abroad, Norton, New York, 2003, and Mann, *op cit.*, 2, 2005. Empirical research shows that these relations are not that simple. In any case, it is clear that a strong correlation exists between economic development and democratic restructuring. Smith, Z.K., The impact of political liberalisation and democratisation on ethnic conflict in Africa: an empirical test of common assumptions, *Journal of Modern African Studies*, 38, 21–39, 2000.

16. Manor, J., op. cit., 22–23, 1989.
17. Zoon, C., *Aymara-Indianen in de Andes op oorlogspad* (Aymara-Indians in the Andes at war), *Volkskrant*, 23 June 2003. At a conference in La Paz (13–15 September 2003), discussions with representatives of the indigenous people clearly indicated that they experience a wide gap between politics and the 'people'.
18. See Wippler, R., *Nicht-intendierte soziale Folgen individueller Handlungen* (Unintended social consequences of individual actions), *Soziale Welt*, 29, 155–179, 1978; Horowitz, D.L., op.cit., 29, 1985.
19. See de Swaan, A., op. cit., Chapter 3, 1989.
20. Scott Bennett, D. and Stam, A.C. III, The duration of interstate wars, 1816–1985, *American Political Science Review*, 90, 239–257, especially pages 242–251, 1996.
21. Hudson, V.M. and Den Boer, A. A surplus of men, a deficit of peace, *International Security*, 5–38, 2002 (26–4). The quantitative study that took this variable into account but could not find a significant result is: Fearon, J.D. and Laitin, D.D., *op. cit.*, 86, 2003.
22. Horowitz, D.L., *op. cit.*, 182, 1985 and Horowitz, D.L., *The Deadly Ethnic Riot*, University of California Press, Berkeley, 55, 2001.
23. Lake D.A. and Rothchild, D., op. cit., 52, 1996.
24. Hodson, R., Sekulic D. and Massey, G., op. cit., 1554–1555, 1994. My interpretation of this paradox is slightly different from the authors'.
25. An analysis of the role of political elites in the former Yugoslavia fighting for power and hence creating ethnic strife can be found in Gagnon, V.P. Jr., Ethnic nationalism and international conflict: the case of Serbia, *International Security*, 19, 130–166, 1994/95.
26. Collins, R., *Weberian Sociological Theory*, Cambridge University Press, Cambridge, 1986, especially Imperialism and legitimacy: Weber's theory of politics, 145–166, and The future decline of the Russian empire, 186–209. The effect of a country's large size on the probability of internal conflicts has been demonstrated in Fearon J.D. and Laitin, D.D., op. cit., 85, 2003. It is interesting to note that as early as 1954, the political scientist Karl Deutsch made a similar prediction with regard to the destiny of the Soviet Union, see Deutsch, K., Cracks in the monolith, in Friedrich, C.J., *Totalitarianism*, Perspective, Cambridge, 308–333, 1954.
27. Collins, R., Prediction in macrosociology: the case of the Soviet collapse, *American Journal of Sociology*, 100, 1552–1593, 1995.

4

VIOLENCE AND (DE)CIVILISATION

This aspect of the origin of violence is connected with the name Norbert Elias. It is rather a tall order to do justice to the very relevant and valuable theory of this renowned sociologist within the scope of this book.[1] Elias focuses on the major development trends in society. He signals some developments in the course of history that are not so much each other's cause and effect but which certainly have a mutual influence on each other.

First, he points to the expansion of the dependency networks referred to in the previous chapter. In the course of time, people have learnt to deal with a continuously growing number of people who live further and further away. One only needs to bear in mind people's life stories that originally — in the Middle Ages and before — took place in small-scale local or regional communities. As the last millennium progressed, the autonomy of small, rival administrative units, such as counties and duchies, was reduced and more large-scale kingdoms and other states came into being. This increased mobility and in their economic and social relations, people were confronted with increasingly larger numbers of other people as well as with different kinds of people.

Nations, often kingdoms, arose because they could anticipate better the possibilities and requirements of the ever-expanding, modernising and internationalising economic and social relations (colonies!). National governments were given many tasks, such as the monopoly on taxation and, more importantly, on violence. The foundation of a central police force and armed forces is closely connected with the rise of nations.[2]

This process of the expanding dependency chain went together with a second major development, i.e. the tendency of societies, as well as of the people in those societies, to become more civilised. In the course of centuries, people have learnt to control their impulses. In the Middle Ages and during the Roman Empire before that, societies were plainly violent. Pillaging and fire-raising armies were on the rampage and, in the struggle of all against all, it was often a matter of kill or be killed. Whoever showed restraint or could not defend themselves was in danger of losing their lives. Hence, there was little control of violence. When administrative expansion took place, enabling a king or prince to subject an entire area to his will, human society, however, gradually grew more peaceful. As was indicated above, exercising violent force was allocated to specialists, such as the military and the police.

At the King's court, on the other hand, new personal characteristics were required, namely good manners, eloquence, as well as diplomatic and administrative skills. Anyone in these circles who took up arms on the slightest provocation was unwelcome. The courtiers had to learn to curb their violent urges and emotions. This process of becoming 'courtly' (the development of controlled conduct) started with the social elite but was gradually imitated by ordinary citizens in the course of centuries; first the retailers and shop owners, later the farmers and labourers. Gradually, people developed a kind of 'self-restraint' (*Selbstzwang*). This self-restraint developed simultaneously, and in combination with, the external restraint (*Fremdkontrolle*) by authorities or persons responsible for the public order in society (teachers at school, bosses at work, the police and the military). However, self-restraint, in comparison with external restraint, has become much more important in the course of time.

People have learnt to control themselves in the company of others so that they can associate smoothly. This is mandatory because in the busy, modern, urbanised societies of today, people have become increasingly dependent on each other. They meet in bureaucratic work situations, at school and on the road. A person who would give in to violent rage, annoyance or impatience while on the road, may run the risk of causing a fatal accident. Persons who cannot control their financial affairs may land in difficulty. A person who thinks he can treat a secretary at work, or anyone else, with disdain, is likely to be sacked very quickly. Nowadays, the father who treats his children in an authoritarian manner should not be surprised if they leave home at an early age. In the last few decades, families have evolved from 'households of command' to 'households of negotiation'.[3]

In all encounters with others, people are forced to deal with each other in a 'decent' manner. They ought to teach themselves self-restraint and to suppress the urge for violent outbursts. This is why, since the Middle Ages, acts of violence have gradually moved more and more into the background of society. Blatant cruelty (torture, maiming) has disappeared from modern Western societies and schools have done away with corporal punishment. Children are no longer beaten at home, while table manners have become more 'civilised' and more hygienic. Women are no longer openly 'grabbed' and people no longer quarrel at the top of their voices. In today's societies, this is simply 'not done' or is punishable by law and sometimes, there is even the prospect of severe sanctions.[4] In general, there is less violence nowadays in the day-to-day relations between people, but this is also true for what goes on between and inside organisations. Violence simply destroys too much in present day society.

If we compare today's society with that of Roman times, the Middle Ages or the nineteenth-century Wild West, then our society is considerably less violent. 'Modern society has seen an abrupt decline in ferocity', wrote Collins.[5] In the past, political differences were usually solved by blood and murder, irrespective of where it happened — as in Rome or Istanbul, in the heyday of the Ottoman Empire. People then could also really 'enjoy' torture and slaughter, presented as a game to a large gathering of spectators (the gladiators in the Colosseum, the jousting tournaments of knights, public executions, the burning of cats and witches).[6] Such 'amusement' has disappeared from modern society altogether. When a publican has a mind to organise a round of 'midget throwing' or 'cage fighting' in his establishment, he will soon find the police on his doorstep. One form of violence as popular entertainment, professional boxing, is still allowed, but only under very strict conditions. In some countries (Scandinavia), professional boxing is already banned whereas in other countries, discussions are going on about this as well. In Spain, bull fighting in its current atrocious form is expected to be in its last decade.

Where violent crime is concerned, historically the picture is no different. In medieval towns, thirty to forty times as many people died violent deaths than in today's society. There was also more frequent physical assault. Apparently medieval society was much less safe and much more dangerous than ours. In more recent times, in the period from 1870 to 1880 to be precise, in the Netherlands, three times as many people were convicted for physical assault than in 1970–1980. Simultaneously, police action had gradually become more effective in that same period. So the police became increasingly effective, but the number of convictions for assault was spectacularly less. Apparently, in the period 1870–1880, there was more violent and cruel behaviour in the streets of the Netherlands than a century later. In Britain, the situation was no different.[7] This should be no surprise when the alcohol-induced pub brawls, murders and open violence during carnival and rowdy village festivals come to mind, that were certainly no exception a hundred years ago. The town of Oss in the Dutch province of Brabant, for example, was notorious for its inhabitants, the so-called 'knife fighters of Oss'. In recent years, after 1970, this image of violent crime has changed somewhat, certainly where blood and murder are concerned, but this will be discussed in greater detail later. This change can be observed both in the Netherlands and in Britain.

Over the centuries, from one generation to the next, a strong dislike of the use of violence has developed. What matters is that it is not just a reduction of violence itself. The tendency towards creating a civilised society has made the definition of what is acceptable violence gradually more restrictive. The present day discussion about sexual harassment of women, currently going so far in the United States that a prolonged stare in the direction of women is likely to be labelled as 'harassment', is a clear illustration.

Nowadays, therapists encounter problems while treating their patients because they are no longer allowed to touch them (especially women and children). These days it is considered to be sexual harassment, that is to say, the undesirable exercise of power or application of violence.[8] The sensitivity about the exertion of violence has gone so far that wringing a stray chicken's neck in a Barcelona football stadium, or French professional football player Cantona throwing an unsuccessful karate kick in the direction of a spectator, is literally world news.[9]

The definition of what is acceptable violence has become considerably curtailed in the course of time. And the revulsion against violence has grown progressively. Nothing much is heard about the more than a thousand victims that die in road accidents in the Netherlands. However, every deadly consequence of what is nowadays called 'senseless violence' causes an enormous uproar all over the country. Still, the number of victims of fatal road accidents is four or five times as many as the annual number of deaths as a result of violence and murder.[10] Nevertheless, any casualty, it must be added, is one too many.

Such an abhorrence of violence, in other words, such inhibition of violence, could arise because people could count on the authorities that are designated to deal with it (the 'monopolists of violence'), especially the police and the military. An indication of this is the reaction of Dutch citizens to meeting places for drug addicts in towns like Rotterdam and Maastricht. Despite the fact that these places ('Platform 0', 'Junkie Park') were unmistakably considered a great nuisance, it never came to confrontations and physical violence between the 'civilised' general public and the junkies. The 'civilised' citizens put pressure on the authorities, which then took measures to reduce the nuisance.

A military example of the control of violence is the introduction of new technologies, aimed at exercising 'violence at a distance'. This happened, for example, in the Gulf War in the shape of what became familiar as 'precision' or 'surgical' bombing. In the years following the war, this technology was developed to even greater perfection. While modernising their arsenal, in general, the Western militaries are constantly searching for cleaner and more precise weapons, which cause less and less bloodshed.[11] In the combat training of new recruits, many a modern Western military has simply dispensed with the bayonet as a weapon.

Comparing the Gulf campaign of 1991 with war in the distant and not so distant past, it is striking to see how 'careful' the military were with human lives during the Gulf War, at least in contrast with the two World Wars and Vietnam. In the latter three wars, huge numbers of human lives were almost carelessly put at stake, and these high numbers were often in no proportion to the intended (military) goals. In comparison, very few American and British soldiers died in the Gulf War or during the military operations in Iraq in 2003 and 2004; until the middle of 2005 the United States forces had suffered a little over 1,700 casualties as compared to some 50,000 casualties during the Vietnam War. Still, every incident in the Iraq operations in which soldiers were killed attracted much attention.

Going further back (ancient history, the history of the Crusades), history reveals even more gruesome examples of the carelessness with which boys and men were sent to their certain deaths. In the course of history, military commanders have been shown to be completely indifferent to the lives of others, particularly when it involved the lives (and deaths) of the enemy, of course. In the golden days of Athens, some 2,500 years ago, prisoners of war were sent to the silver mines where they were forced to stay until they died. During the Crusades, the practice of impalement — skewering enemies on a long spit or spear — evolved, sometimes leading to 'spectacular' sights of 20,000 corpses hanging on sharpened stakes outside the walls of a captured city.[12] However, in the course of history, there was also negligence regarding the life and death of slaves, the blacks or the working class youth, who could very well serve as cannon fodder for the good cause. The perception of military commanders of the limited value of the life of an enemy and that of their own troops finds its pendant in the way in which nineteenth-century employers thought about their work force and colonials about the natives.

All this has changed, fortunately. Currently, casualty aversion among the general public and military personnel is one of the major concerns of politicians and generals who want to go to war. This illustrates again how much the sensitivity about violence and manslaughter has increased in modern societies. Interestingly enough, the ambition to use as little violence as possible is not caused by concern about one's own 'boys and girls' only. Brutal violence against others (even if it is the enemy) is no longer accepted either. We must recall the resignation of the Bolivian government and top military officers after the killing of some 100 protesters in the streets of La Paz in October 2003, or the self-restraining behaviour of the United States forces in the streets of Baghdad and other Iraqi cities, when they were operating in the vicinity of religious monuments.

Violence in less civilised states

The gist of all this is that in those areas where there are violent outbursts (Rwanda, Somalia, Bosnia, the Congo, etc.), the 'level of civilisation' is less well developed than in modern, stable states. This is not exactly a politically correct statement, but there certainly are good arguments supporting this observation.

According to Elias' theory, internal outbursts of violence are restrained due to an efficient government exercising an effectively functioning monopoly of force (police and military). In the areas where such outbursts take place (Rwanda, etc.), what strikes the observer first and foremost is the absence of a well-functioning central government. They are so-called 'failed states' without a central government that can provide an effective and just use of violence, to prevent the situation from getting worse. As was described in previous chapters, conflicts arise where there is power vacuum, political anarchy and ethnic nepotism (favouring members of one's own group). Nothing is as damaging as using an army or police force exclusively against certain population groups, and intentionally not against other groups (as happened in the former Yugoslavia, Rwanda and on many occasions in India and other regions in the Far East).

However, violence also has to do with 'self-restraint' and an inhibition to use violence, which does not seem so well developed and refined in these areas yet. The skills to control affects and emotions such as anger, retaliation and revenge are not so highly developed. In this respect, a very telling comparison can be made between the unrestrained violence used by the Russians against the Chechen capital of Grozny in 1994 and the comparatively limited exercise of violence in the 1991 Gulf War or the war in Iraq in 2003 by the United States and the UK. But then Russia, it has to be added, is still a nation with a relatively civilised reputation!

In what we call 'less civilised states', people are used to dealing with each other in a harsher way. They have less compassion for themselves and for others and show less self-control. In short, during conflicts, people are used to treating each other in a harsher, more violent and perhaps also more cruel manner. A human life is simply worth less, or to put it differently, life seems cheap. There are numerous examples of this phenomenon. An example of 'barbarity towards oneself' comes from the Lebanon, where Shiites have ritual methods of self-castigation. As a manner of initiation, young men use machetes to inflict serious head wounds on themselves.[13] In many countries in the Middle East weapons are fired in the air to express joy, as a result of which hospitals have their hands full treating the many wounded afterwards. During the Taliban regime in Afghanistan, offences such as thieving and committing adultery were punished by cutting off hands. The conduct of a legal case and the argumentation in such trials was very primitive in the eyes of Westerners — only a few witness accounts usually sufficed for the sentencing and carrying out of the actual punishment. Muslim terrorists mock non-Muslims because they love their life too much, which, as they say, makes them unfit to fight.[14] In many other regions in the world (the Caucasus, Africa, Haiti), killing as a way to solve problems is still common practice.

But in Europe also, in the former Yugoslavia, this phenomenon seemed to play a role. Most Serbs, even the *fini ljudi*, the 'fine people' from the larger cities, such as Novi Sad, had originally come from the rough, rural countryside only one generation earlier.[15] There, the outlook on life, on animals, on women, and on each other, was totally different. As Ugresic describes it, the denigrating manner in which men in the former Yugoslavia approached

46

women is absolutely shocking to Westerners.[16] And where else than in the former Yugoslavia does it happen that a dog is left to die by the side of the road for three miserable days on end? In this perspective, it is not so strange that this 'uncouth' population group is capable of committing serious acts of violence. They have only had a relatively short period of time to experience the civilisation process, which Western Europe went through at length, so they have not been able to 'internalise' a sufficient measure of self-restraint. It is therefore not entirely coincidental that communal violence seems to occur primarily in rural communities of peasants and shepherds, or to put it in general geographic terms, in mountainous terrain, as a large-scale quantitative study has demonstrated.[17] Therefore, the violence in the former Yugoslavia is seemingly all about the return of the 'savage inhabitant', which is also the reason why Els de Temmerman yelled furiously at murderers in Rwanda, 'The whole world thinks you are savages!'[18]

This train of thought, however, is not without opposition. Anthropologist Mattijs van de Port elaborates on this reasoning, but at the same time, he warns against drawing the wrong conclusions. In his opinion, the difference between 'civilisation' and an 'unrestrained warlike nature', between 'us-the-civilised' and 'them-the-barbarians', is just a thin layer that can easily be 'scraped off'.[19] In certain circumstances, everybody can lapse into violent action under the pressure of micro processes, which will be referred to later.

When leaders have led the way in committing acts of violence, others are tempted to do the same. Once the followers have given in to committing violence, then there is no way back, neither psychologically nor legally. This is the reason why one-time offenders are bolstered in what they do and violence escalates. An atmosphere of violence arises in which even very ordinary people become callous and indifferent towards violence and start to consider it as part of everyday existence.[20] These processes will be discussed later in the chapter on the dynamics of conflict.

Every person can get entangled in such a process, even the 'peaceful' Dutch, as the experiences of the police actions in the former Dutch East Indies in the 1940s testify. During UN peace support operations, violence can get out of control, as happened to Belgian and Canadian blue helmets in Somalia in 1994. Another indication is a Dutch newspaper article reporting on the collective application for a weapon licence by two hundred inhabitants of Lunteren, a small town in the province of Gelderland. The residents wanted to arm themselves against burglars sweeping the village. They were most dissatisfied with the response of the police, who were badly affected by recent budget cuts. The inhabitants therefore decided to take the law into their own hands.[21] In Maluku, an archipelago belonging to Indonesia, groups of militant civilians got involved in the deadly conflicts between Christians and Muslims that have occurred since 1999, because 'the government was not fulfilling its role in protecting the people'. And hence, those militants were 'replacing government.'[22] The hostage taking in a

47

school in Beslan in North Ossetia in September 2004 had a dramatic outcome, with hundreds of deaths, because civilians — parents whose children were imprisoned in the school — started firing at the rebels, whereupon chaos developed and the military was forced to intervene. Clearly, this catastrophe in South Russia was not anticipated in the armed forces' plan to end the crisis.[23] In Chechnya, unemployed males were in possession of heavy arms, which they used to 'restore justice' by seizing the apartments and other property owned mainly by ethnic Russians.[24]

These incidents show that an effectively operating central government is a condition *sine qua non* for a 'civilised intercourse' between people. The central authority (police and judiciary) must possess the required tools and go about their business in a professional, incorruptible way. If this is not so, when the necessity increases, all people, even in the modernised and so-called civilised societies, could lose their restraint. Violence may then arise, comparable with what has become customary in various cities in the United States today. It is not without reason that the violence in the ghettos of some major cities of the United States or South and Central America (especially Brazil) has been likened to the acts of war in Bosnia.[25]

The control of violence in various situations

So far, the following ideas have been made clear in this chapter. In modern societies with an adequately functioning monopoly of violence, the inclination to resort to violence is increasingly suppressed. In societies that are not yet (completely) modernised and civilised, the tendency to control violence is less strongly developed. This phenomenon may lead to internal outbursts of violence in such countries, especially in a 'failing state' (a state with an inadequately functioning monopoly of violence). These situations are shown in Figure 4. In this figure, the process of affect and violence control has been represented as an 'upward' spiral. However, the level of violence control varies.

The following deductions can be made on the basis of the figure:

- In agreement with Elias' theory, there is a long-term development aimed at violence control. The upward directed arrows at the bottom of the spiral indicate this long-term trend. Important elements are a monopoly of violence which functions effectively and an extensive system of mutual dependencies (the latter means a situation in which people can rely on others to behave well and in a controlled manner because otherwise, living together would be impossible, e.g. in traffic).
- In different situations, the level of violence control varies. Modern societies with a more stable monopoly of violence and in which people

48

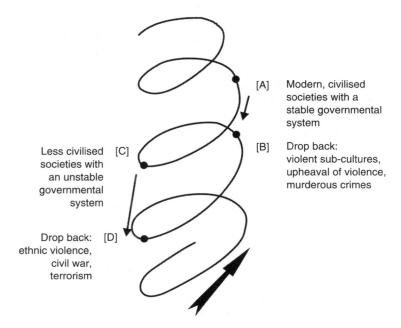

[A]   Modern, civilised societies with a stable governmental system

[B]   Drop back: violent sub-cultures, upheaval of violence, murderous crimes

Less civilised [C] societies with an unstable governmental system

Drop back: [D] ethnic violence, civil war, terrorism

Figure 4 Spiral showing different situations with increasing and decreasing control of violence.

have learnt to control themselves because otherwise life would be impossible, have a relatively high level of violence control, indicated as [A].

- There does not necessarily have to be a constantly upward movement towards violence control — a temporary or permanent drop is possible just as well. In the theory, this is referred to as decivilisation.[26] This is indicated by the two arrows pointing downward from [A] to [B] and from [C] to [D]. Two hundred years of crime in New York shows that the city has had three waves of violence, which have been put to a stop each time. Obviously there are waves of violence that come and go.[27] [B] and [D] show that the tendency towards violence control can drop back in all types of societies. It is important to realise that in various violent conflicts in the 'less civilised states' (Rwanda, Bosnia, the Congo and others; indicated as [D]), often relatively small groups of unhinged youth and men are responsible for the dismal state of affairs. In Rwanda, for example, these youth were the Interahamwe, militias of unemployed and sometimes HIV-infected Hutus, who had nothing to lose. Those militias, originating from soccer fan clubs, were primarily responsible for the many murders and rapes.[28] In Bosnia, the (para)

49

military units such as the Serbian Tigers, who had gone completely astray, had a considerable share in the atrocities. However widespread outbursts of violence may be, there are always some that allow themselves to behave worse than others.

- That a decline of violence control also occurs in the civilised West is borne out by the situation around fringe groups, such as dropouts, football hooligans and criminals. This is indicated by [B], signifying a drop back in violence control as compared to [A]. The background of their behaviour is the lesser need for self-control, because these groups often participate to a lesser degree in the previously described network branches (family, school, work, formerly also conscription). They are more or less excluded from the normal social intercourse between people.[29] At the same time, unhinged youth continue to feel the need for social protection; this can be achieved by forming gangs, which could be called an expression of present day tribalism.[30] In these gangs, a subculture may develop, in which the gang-members 'lust for violence', as it were. The rise of such a violent culture is enhanced by 'role models' from the world of video games and films such as *The Terminator Man*. Moreover, it appears that, in general, the inclination towards violence control in Western societies is less strong these days as compared to some twenty or thirty years ago. Hence, more violence in everyday life seems to have developed in Western societies over the last two or three decades. Besides this, a form of social contagion is also possible — there are clear indications that criminal circles in the Netherlands are getting more violent as a consequence of the arrival of people from the former Yugoslavia in particular (the so-called Yugo scene). These people, who have come from a war situation, do not shy away from using heavy violence, which in turn is copied by 'indigenous' Dutch criminals. In general, [B] must be taken as an indication of the real situation with regard to the occurrence of violence in the Netherlands and the UK since 1970, a situation which has progressively deteriorated.[31]

- The rate of movement along the spiral — up as well as down — may differ according to period and cultural or geographic area. It is likely that the process of violence control takes place over a time span of some centuries, while a drop back may happen more quickly. As always, the building up takes longer than the breaking down.

These conclusions illustrate that the dynamics of the control of violence develop as a macro process, spanning a period of centuries. However, there are also short periods of movements at micro level in the opposite direction. The conclusions put the all too simple belief in the superiority of the so-called civilised societies into its proper perspective. Despite the tendency towards civilisation described by Elias, there will always be the possibility that violence control in modernised and civilised societies will collectively fail. In this respect, the recollection of the holocaust says enough. Chapter 6 will go into this at some length.

Notes

1. A clear introduction to the work of Norbert Elias is St. Mennell, op. cit., 1992. Other discussions of his work can be found in Fletcher, J., *Violence and Civilization*, Polity Press, Cambridge, 1997; Opp, K.D., *Die Entstehung Sozialer Normen (The Origins of Social Norms)*, J.C.B. Mohr Verlag, Tübingen, 149–175, 1983; de Swaan, A., *De Mensenmaatschappij. Een Inleiding (Human Society. An Introduction)*, Bert Bakker, Amsterdam, 1996.
2. Tilly, Ch., *Coercion, Capital and European states. AD 990–1990*, Blackwell, Cambridge, 1992.
3. de Swaan, A., op. cit., 70–71, 1996.
4. For a historical-sociological review of developments in cruelty and violence, the reader is referred to Collins, R., Three faces of cruelty: towards a comparative sociology of violence, *Theory and Society*, 1, 415–440, 1974. A historical review of developments in corporal punishment and torture is Ryley Scott, G., *The History of Torture*, Bracken Books, London, 1995. See also Elias, N., On tranformations of aggressiveness, *Theory and Society*, 5, 219–228, 1978.
5. Collins, R., op. cit., 431, 1974.
6. About ancient Rome, see for instance, Meijer, F., *Keizers Sterven niet in Bed (Emperors Do not Die in Bed)*, Atheneum, Amsterdam, 2001 and Meijer, F., *Gladiatoren. Volksvermaak in het Colosseum (Gladiators. Popular Entertainment in the Colosseum)*, Atheneum, Amsterdam, 2003.
7. Franke, H., *Geweldscriminaliteit in Nederland. Een historisch-sociologische analyse* (Violent crime in the Netherlands. A historical-sociological analysis), in Franke, H., Wilterdink N. and Brinkgreve, C., (eds.), *Alledaags en ongewoon geweld* (Everyday and Unusual Violence), *Amsterdams Sociologisch Tijdschrift*, 13–45, in particular, 16–23, 1991.
8. Brandt, E., *Spanning in de spreekkamer* (Tension in the consultation room), *Volkskrant*, 4 January 1997, p.7.
9. Both events happened in January 1995. The incident with Cantona took place in England.
10. These statistics can be found in Hogerwerf, A., *Geweld in Nederland (Violence in the Netherlands)*, Van Gorcum, Assen, 11, 1996; Leistra G. and Nieuwbeerta, P., *Tien Jaar Moord en Doodslag in Nederland (Ten Years of Murder and Homicide in the Netherlands)*, Prometheus, Amsterdam, 2003.
11. Toffler, A. and Toffler, H., *War and Anti-War. Survival at the Dawn of the 21st Century*, Bantam, New York, 1994; see also Soeters, J., The Dutch military and the use of violence, *Netherlands' Journal of Social Sciences*, 37, 24–37, 2001.
12. See Dixon, N.F., *On the Psychology of Military Incompetence*, Futura, London, 1991; Walzer, M., op. cit., 1992. See also Wheatcroft, A., *Infidels. A History of the Conflict between Christendom and Islam*, Penguin Books, London, especially page 206, 2004.

13. van Amerongen, A. and Schreur, E., *Duizend liter verspild bloed in Nabatija* (Thousand litres of spilt blood in Nabatija), *Vrij Nederland*, 48–52, 15 July 1995.
14. Stern, J., *Terror in the Name of God. Why Religious Militants Kill*, Harper Collins, New York, 125, 2003.
15. van de Port, M., *Het Einde van de Wereld. Beschaving, Redeloosheid en Zigeunercafes in Servië (The End of the World. Civilization, Irrationality, and Gipsy Bars in Serbia)*, Babylon/de Geus, Amsterdam, 1994.
16. Ugresic, D., op. cit., especially Chapter 'For we are boys', page 149ff, 1995.
17. Laitin, D.D., National revivals and violence, *European Journal of Sociology*, 36, 3–43, in particular pages 14ff, 1995. A similar observation can be found in Faber, M., op. cit., 101 and 124, 2001. The anthropologist Anton Blok has shown that Mafia violence has its origin in rural villages: Blok, A., *Honour and Violence*, Polity Press, Cambridge, 2001. The quantitative study is Fearon J.D. and Laitin, D.D., op. cit., 85, 2003, page 85.
18. de Temmerman, E., op. cit., 51, 1994.
19. van de Port, M., *Wat bezielt die mensen toch* (What ever has come over those people)? *Volkskrant*, 11 January 1995. In his book about Elias' work (*see* endnote 1) St. Mennell devotes an extensive discussion on the real or supposed ethnocentrism in the work of Elias. See Chapter 10 of that book in particular. That chapter has been the source of inspiration for the remainder of this section.
20. Laitin, D., op. cit., 1995. An analysis of the excesses during the Dutch police actions in the then Dutch East Indies can be found in van Doorn J.A.A. and Hendrix. W.J., op. cit., 1970.
21. Anonymous, *Burgers vragen om wapens bij actie tegen criminaliteit* (Civilians ask for weapons to use in action against crime), *Volkskrant*, 12 January 1995.
22. J. Stern, op. cit., 70, 2003.
23. Anonymous, Russian media: civilians shot first, ANP/Reuters, 7 September 2004.
24. Tishkov, V., op. cit., 585, 1999.
25. Enzensberger, H.M., op. cit., 1994. Interesting in this connection is a report by Holtwijk, I., Moordstad (Murderous city), *Volkskrant*, 25 February 1995, about the most violent city in the world, Rio de Janeiro. In this report, it becomes clear that the police in Rio are part of the problem. Twenty percent of the military police and 70% of the ordinary police are corrupt. Not surprisingly, crime is most prevalent during the night, when the police are usually not present. See Melbin, M., Night as frontier, *American Sociological Review*, 43, 3–22, 1972. See also Wacquant, L.J.D., *Decivilisering en diabolisering. De transformatie van het Amerikaanse zwarte getto* (Decivilisation and demonising. The transformation of the American black ghetto), *Amsterdams Sociologisch Tijdschrift*, 24, 320–348, 1997. Also the current kidnapping 'industry' in Mexico is at least partly related to malfunctioning and corrupt police forces.
26. See also Mennell, S., Short-term interests and long-term processes: the case of civilisation and decivilisation, in Goudsblom, J., Jones E.L. and St. Mennell, *Human History and Social Process*, University of Exeter Press, Exeter, 93–127, 1989.

27. Schuyt, C.J.M., *Tweehonderd jaar stedelijk geweld* (Two hundred years of urban violence), *Delikt en Delinkwent*, 31, 785–791, 2001.
28. See de Temmerman, E., op. cit., 1994; Gourevitch, Ph., op. cit., 93 and 115, 1998; Human Rights Watch, annual reports, 1995.
29. For example, Dunning, E.G., Murphy P. and Williams, J., *The Roots of Football Hooliganism: An Historical and Sociological Study*, Routledge, London, 1988. Also, see Staub, E., Cultural-societal roots of violence. The examples of genocidal violence and of comtemporary youth violence in the United States, *American Psychologist*, 117–132, 1996; Enzensberger, H.M., op. cit., 1994.
30. Maffesoli, M., *The Time of the Tribes*, Sage, London, 1996.
31. van den Brink G. and Schuyt, K., *Van kwaad tot erger. Wordt geweld nu ook gedemocratiseerd?* (From bad to worse. Is violence now also being democratised?), *Mens en Maatschappij*, 77, 7–17, 2002; about violent crime among migrant people, Bovenkerk, F., *Misdaadprofielen (Profiles of Crime)*, Meulenhoff, Amsterdam, 2001.

5

VIOLENCE AND CULTURE

In Scandinavian countries, the law forbids professional boxing, and in other Western European countries there are discussions about such a law, while in the United States, the same sport is big business. In one country, defence expenditure is several times the amount of money other countries are willing to spend for this purpose. Often the latter category makes relatively more money available as aid to developing countries. What causes these differences and is there any link with the rise of violence and conflict? The answer to this question has to do with the differences between national cultures, which indeed have a presumably large influence on the rise of conflict and violence in the world. So, whereas the emphasis in the foregoing chapter was on the historical development of violence, in the present chapter, we deal with the varying levels of violence originating from current differences between national cultures. This focus has become important since the famous political scientist Samuel Huntington announced that the world was going to see a 'clash of civilisations'. In other publications, he has also emphasised the importance of cultures and values in explaining developments in the world.[1]

In order to understand how national cultures lie at the root of violence and conflict, it may be helpful to gain an insight into the work of Dutch social scientist Geert Hofstede.[2] He has been able to establish differences between national cultures by using so-called value standards of more than 100,000 respondents in over 50 countries. The underlying idea was that culture — 'collective mental programming'— can be represented by the opinions of people about the fundamental aspects of life and work. People have acquired these values and opinions in their formative years, which are the years between the 'sociological birth' (at circa one year) and the beginning of their maturity (roughly at the age of 20). After this age, these fundamental opinions hardly change anymore. This is the reason why stable differences arise between groups of people in the way in which they look at the various 'questions of life'. These different 'orientations of life', the crux of understanding culture, can be recognised in the way people behave in various kinds of circumstances. These differences manifest

54

themselves clearly at the national level, as has been demonstrated by Hofstede.

He has proved that the differences in values between countries can be reduced to five cultural dimensions. These cultural features of countries were formed over the centuries and are relatively stable, as has also been shown in other, more recent studies.[3] These cultural dimensions can be associated with many questions of social order and development, four of which are of importance in the explanation of the rise of conflict and violence.

Tough–soft

First, there is the dimension of masculinity and femininity, or tough and soft. This dimension is about the importance attached to achievement and material wealth. It is found in, among other things, the appreciation of the following matters:

- rewarding of the strong versus solidarity with the weak
- economic growth versus care for the environment
- expenditure on armament versus development aid.[4]

Masculine cultures aspire to a tough, achievement-oriented society, in which 'going for gold' and 'the winner takes it all' are popular expressions. Feminine cultures, on the other hand, stress the importance of prosperity for all, the quality of life, the environment and mutual solidarity. In feminine countries, the roles of men and women in society overlap — both genders are relatively modest and aimed at co-operation. In masculine countries, there are important differences between how men and women function in society — men are expected to be dominant, ambitious and tough, whereas women are expected to be modest and focussed on a relationship. In masculine countries, taxes are lower than in feminine countries; in feminine countries, in order to protect the weak, much is done about the redistribution of wealth by way of social security and development aid. Examples of masculine countries are Japan, Austria, Italy, Ireland, Great Britain, Germany, the United States and Mexico; distinct examples of feminine countries are the Scandinavian countries and the Netherlands.

There is much to be said about the many implications of this dimension. When concentrating on the subject of violence and conflict, the following is of importance. First, in countries with a masculine culture, there is more political violence. This effect is unrelated to other factors such as population size and economic development.[5] In addition, the volume of defence expenditure is statistically connected with masculinity. The more masculine the culture, the larger the part of the national budget that goes to defence and the armed forces. This connection also applies to the poor

55

countries that receive support from other countries for their defence policy. Masculine countries are more inclined to solve conflicts by fighting and military actions (the UK in Northern Ireland, the USA and the UK in Iraq), whereas feminine countries will try to do so by negotiating and making compromises.

An illustrative example of this assertion is a comparison between the course of events at the time of the so-called Aland crisis and the Falklands crisis. The Aland group is a small archipelago situated between Sweden and Finland. When Finland received its independence from Russia in 1917, the majority of the population wanted the islands to be part of Sweden as, earlier in history, they had already been Swedish territory. The Fins arrested the leaders of the pro-Swedish movement, after which fierce and highly emotional negotiations followed. This eventually resulted in a solution which was acceptable to all parties — the islands became a Finnish region, but with a high degree of regional autonomy. Since then, the Aland island group has become a prosperous area.

This is in shrill contrast with the course of the so-called Falklands crisis. The Falklands Islands, situated off the Argentine coast, have been a British colony since 1833, but Argentina has claimed the rights to the islands since 1767. In 1982, the Argentine military occupied the islands, which are only very thinly populated. The British Government, under the leadership of the Iron Lady, Margaret Thatcher, immediately sent a veritable armada to the South Atlantic and the invaders were soon repulsed. But it happened at a cost — officially 725 Argentine and 225 British lives were lost. Additionally, it had a huge impact on the government finances of both nations. The economy of the islands was completely destroyed by the war, trade with the Argentine hinterland became impossible and the Argentines have still not relinquished their claims to the area. The problem is still simmering and will no doubt erupt another day.[6] In the Falklands crisis, two masculine cultures were poised, while in the Aland crisis, two feminine cultures. It would be interesting as a thought experiment to ponder over the question of what the feminine, negotiation- and consensus-oriented Netherlands would do in the event of an occupation by masculine Venezuela of the Dutch Antilles, lying off its coast.

What is foreign is dangerous

The second relevant cultural dimension in Hofstede's research is the avoidance of uncertainty. This dimension refers to the question of how people cope with uncertain and unfamiliar situations.[7] If the inclination to avoid uncertainty in a country is relatively weak, then people feel at ease in these kinds of situations and will not develop any feelings of fear and violent emotions (distrust, nationalism). Moreover, no measures will be taken to prevent these situations. If, however, the inclination to avoid uncertainty is relatively large in a country, then people will soon become nervous and emotional when new, uncertainty-inducing situations occur. Then, everything possible will be done to counter or prevent these situations, for example, by issuing many and meticulous rules, laws and bans, and by obliging people to go by the book in everything they do. Ambiguity is rejected, deviation is ridiculed and criticised overtly, and in the most severe cases, misdemeanour is punished through ostracism and public flogging.

For the subjects of violence and conflict, it is of special importance that people in uncertainty-avoiding cultures are inclined to reject others in general and strangers in particular. Hatred of strangers and racism are more widespread in uncertainty-avoiding countries than elsewhere. Uncertainty avoidance is tersely described in the expression 'what is different and strange, is dangerous'. In Hofstede's study, Greece scored the highest of all countries on this dimension, and it currently happens to be the most racist country in the European Union in terms of policies against immigrants and opinions of the general public.[8] Racism and nationalism find a fertile breeding ground in cultures with a strong avoidance of uncertainty, which is even more reinforced when in combination with a high measure of masculinity. It is not surprising that the Axis powers in the Second World War — Germany, Austria, Japan and Italy — were not only characterised by a high degree of masculinity but also by a relatively high or average degree of uncertainty avoidance (Japan, high; Italy, Austria and Germany, about average). In the ideology of the moment, fear of, and related to that, hatred of strangers (Bolsheviks, Plutocrats, Westerners) and outsiders (Jews) was an important element. Since then, however, these countries are no longer inclined to engage in offensive military action, which may be seen as an attempt to cope with the memories of the atrocities that they were involved in during the 1940s.[9]

Uncertainty avoidance, collectivism and power distance

The third relevant dimension is collectivism/individualism. In collectivist countries, thinking in terms of groups is dominant. In terms of the group grid model, discussed in Chapter 2, in collectivist cultures, there is a preoccupation with group boundaries and distinctions. The collective (the family, the region, the political or religious movement, the football club) is important. In the opposite, usually in the more individualist countries in the West, people are much more self-centred. They do belong to groups but not exclusively to a single group. Voting behaviour, for example, is not identical with a certain group membership. This can be seen in individualist Belgium, where the Flemish and Walloons vote for the Socialists, the Christian Democrats as well as the Liberals. If Belgium had a strong collectivist culture, then every Flemish voter would vote for the only Flemish party and every inhabitant of the Walloon provinces for the only Walloon party. That would seriously endanger the peace and quiet in the country.[10]

Collectivism combined with uncertainty avoidance characterises countries where the government and the administration can only deal with conflicts in an inflexible manner. Minorities are assimilated under great pressure or simply suppressed. They have to blend into the large collective of the nation. Conflicts between groups in these countries soon turn violent because the various minority groups often show the same basic attitude of uncertainty avoidance towards collectivism. From a cultural respect, it does not really matter very much what 'party' is in power in these countries. Examples of countries to which the combination of the two cultural dimensions applies, are among others: Iran, Turkey, various Arab countries, Israel, many African countries and the former Yugoslavia. In almost all these countries, the type of internal conflict, civil opposition and terrorism discussed in this book has been the order of the day for decades.

Again, the name of the former Yugoslavia has come up. It is remarkable that various 'parties' in this disintegrated country — Serbia, Croatia, Bosnia and Slovenia — have the same cultural profile. They are all characterised by a high degree of uncertainty avoidance, combined with a very high degree of collectivism. In addition, they all show a very large power distance, which is the fourth relevant cultural dimension. Power distance refers to the differences between superiors and subordinates, the differences between the elite and ordinary people, and the extent to which these differences are experienced and accepted as normal.[11]

In societies with a large power distance, as in the former Yugoslavia, the powerful in society, the landowners as well as the governmental and the economic elite, are in charge. Those who have the power (and often want more) are not contradicted; the population would not even dare. The mutual enmity in this part of Europe therefore seems to be a constant. The analysis of sociologist Tomasic with regard to society in the Balkans, published in 1946, sounds surprisingly up-to-date. 'Therefore, rivalries and hostilities are paralleled by attachment and subservience to those in power — a situation that breeds both treachery and loyalty, feud and solidarity, factionalism and ethnocentrism, a general feeling of insecurity of life and property, and endless strife. "He who has no enemies is not a man", they say. These are the conditions which made Balkan herdsmen excel in violence, villainy and rebelliousness, as well as in deeds of self-denial and patriotism.'[12]

Tomasic's quotation, published almost sixty years ago, contains all the characteristics of the explosive combination of cultural aspects (power distance, uncertainty avoidance and collectivism) found by Hofstede. How striking this combination of cultural features is, becomes clear from a comparison with another European country where large-scale changes in the economy and the state's administrative system have taken place in a relatively short period of time. This country is Belgium, where the relations between the 'ethnic' groups (the Walloons, the Flemish and the German-speaking Belgians) have completely turned over in the course of a few decades. If, some thirty years ago, the Walloons were the most dominant group in an economic and administrative sense, they have now completely lost that powerful and advantageous position. Yet all these changes have taken place without any bloodshed. While in the former Yugoslavia, social and economic changes could come about only by way of a total internal war, these matters took place in Belgium predominantly through consultation and negotiation (strong grid dynamics) and under the influence of less dominant group dynamics. The latter aspect points at a high level of individualism. This is the only significant difference in cultural profile between the Belgians (Walloon and Flemish) and the population groups in the former Yugoslavia. In both Belgium and the former Yugoslavia, the culture of all population groups has relatively strong features of uncertainty avoidance and power distance. However, Belgium has a low degree of collectivism (and therefore, a high level of individualism), whereas Serbs, Croats and Slovenes have an extremely high level of collectivism (and a low level of individualism) as a cultural characteristic.[13]

This Yugoslav combination of cultural features, which apparently predisposes the area to hostility conflict and violence, is not unique in the population groups in that part of the Balkans. This cultural profile applies to the entire former Byzantine area, including Russia, Greece and Turkey.[14] Greece has the largest uncertainty avoidance of Europe, as we saw earlier, to an even greater extent than the population groups in the former Yugoslavia. A clear manifestation of this cultural feature was Greece's awkward stance when the Netherlands and other EU members recognised the independence of Macedonia, one of the republics of the former Yugoslavia. Part of Northern Greece is another Macedonia and obviously, the Greeks feared the secession of 'their' Macedonia as a result of the independence of Macedonia that was part of the former Yugoslavia. A boycott of Dutch products, encouraged by a popular Greek radio station, was the result!

In this respect, Greece's neighbour Turkey is rather similar. When political-religious riots broke out in Istanbul in March 1995, the Government issued a statement inferring that Greece was behind them. For decades NATO partners Greece and Turkey have squabbled over Cyprus and maritime borders and this constitutes a serious threat to the peace in the area. Recently, in 2003, a UN peace plan for Cyprus failed due to the parties' obstinacy. For more than forty years, no solution had been possible, but even then, despite the presence of UN Secretary General Mr. Kofi Annan and pressure from the EU, the conflict could not be brought to an end. On the other hand, the measure of masculinity in the two countries, Greece and Turkey, is not inordinately high. This situation, in combination with the NATO and EU regimes under which both countries (hope to) operate, fortunately dampens any inclination towards war.[15] This explains why in times of disasters, e.g. earthquakes, both countries are increasingly inclined to support each other.

Comments

Hofstede's work is particularly relevant in the analysis of conflicts between humans. However, these views and insights about national (or regional) cultures are so powerful that there is a dangerous temptation to turn everything into absolute truths. Therefore, the reader should apply these insights when taking the following comments into account.

- Cultural features have to do with collectivities; in this case, they are national populations. It is methodologically and morally unjust to apply cultural features, which derive their meaning from the collective, to individuals. Statistically, Hofstede's data are central tendencies, or average values, which have a larger or smaller distribution. There are, for instance, enough Germans who are more Dutch than the average Dutchmen and vice versa. There are also enough women who run faster than men, whereas on average, men as a category normally run faster than women.

- Not much can be said with absolute certainty about the change of cultural features. Hofstede's findings originate from 1970 and his research has often been replicated in a more or less comparable way.[16] By and large, all these measurements show the same results. In addition, the measurements of cultural features correlate in the same way with numerous national statistical indicators. Moreover, many of Hofstede's results correspond with historical views. All this supports the thought that the insights of Hofstede are remarkably stable and may apply to processes that have been going on for centuries. This may be so to a certain degree, but there are bound to be a number of changes, culturally.

- In any case, the tendency towards individualisation, that is to say the tendency towards less collectivism, has a worldwide impact, which is connected with modernisation and the expansion of prosperity. Globalisation and 'McDonaldisation' (MTV inclusive) also lead to a certain worldwide cultural uniformisation in the field of work and organisation, market dynamics, advertising, music and sports. However, as a reaction to the uniforming tendencies of globalisation, many countries try to incorporate their own cultural character in what is referred to as 'glocalisation'. This means that the 'global' and the 'local' are forged together into something new — a shopping mall after the American example in Ankara retains so many Turkish features (Turkish products, Turkish music) that something new develops, which is different from the original shopping malls in the United States. Glocalisation leads to the preservation of local characteristics within the context of worldwide global standards. This means that the cultural diversity remains emphatically intact, which has been borne out by the numerous follow-ups on Hofstede's research. However, the reaction to globalisation may also be more radical (Figure 5) — in some countries there is a tendency towards modernisation (in terms of adopting technological innovations such as the Internet), going side by side with a total rejection of other Western achievements. Various culture related conflicts, the recent terrorist attacks and the way in which they happened, all too clearly show this two-sidedness (modernising without Westernising). Religious identity often plays an important role in this, as will be shown later on.[17]

- In the analysis of conflicts, cultural factors play an important role, but other aspects such as economic interests, ambitions of power, etc. may naturally not be discarded. Complex problems such as the rise of

Figure 5 Postcard from Kosovo, with a message rejecting globalisation.

violence and conflict can only be understood if insights and approaches are combined.

- The cultural dimensions of Hofstede represent general patterns which may already be centuries old. However, it is possible that nations do things that deviate from the 'dictates' of their cultural pattern. For the Netherlands, for instance, this is true of the explanation of the decolonisation of the 'Dutch East Indies'. For centuries, the Netherlands has had a history of relatively limited violent action, global idealism and distancing itself from power politics.[18] This pattern is in total agreement with the characterisation of the Netherlands as a feminine country. Nevertheless, at the end of the 1940s — albeit it with the best (feminine?) intentions — the Netherlands reacted in a rather constrained and belligerent manner to the aspirations of independence of the Indonesians. So far that has been an unsolved conundrum, certainly when it is compared with the relatively smooth way in which masculine Britain had departed from India, shortly before that.

Just as with any other *grand theory*, it seems wise to apply Hofstede's culture method with care.

Cultures of honour

There is more to say about the connection between culture and violence. Some people argue that certain specific African cultural elements are likely to lead to violence because they stress that death is a source of life. This thought occurs in the so-called rebirth culture in which corpses are shaped so that they lie curled in the same position as a foetus. In this cultural logic, funeral rites are so closely associated with pregnancy that birth, death and rebirth are seen as the elements of one powerful equation.[19]

Surveying the connection between culture and violence, there is still one more important matter. This phenomenon seems to be worldwide and it starts with the observation that in some countries — and in some cultural groups within countries — there is more blood and murder than in other countries and communities. Although violence has clearly increased in the Netherlands since 1970, it is still a relatively safe country with regard to the risk of losing one's life as a result of murder or violence. In many countries, e.g. Scotland, the United States and Mexico, the chance of getting killed due to violence is much larger.[20] About one-fifth of all the cases of blood and murder are instances of taking the life of one's partner — murders that take place in a steady relationship or marriage. In the Netherlands, people from Turkey, Morocco, Surinam or the Antilles run the risk of being murdered by their steady partners at a rate of six to seven times higher than average.[21] For centuries, inhabitants of the southern states of the United States run a much greater risk of getting involved in violence (and die as a result) than inhabitants of the north. In general, Southerners in the United States are more accepting of violence used for coercion and punishment.[22] What do these observations refer to?

Without doubt, poverty and possession of arms have a bearing on the explanation of these phenomena. In a cultural respect, however, the 'honour' factor plays a significant role. As a consequence of often rather trivial occurrences, people, usually men, may feel treated unfairly. They are offended by events that are really trifling, for instance, an insult. These occurrences may have a more profound effect, e.g. a partner's adultery, or a son or daughter's love relationship with somebody belonging to a 'wrong' family. Due to such an event, a personal reputation or the honour of a family may be at stake, which demands revenge and retribution, possibly leading to blood and murder. This is called honour feud, which is a phenomenon that usually occurs in the Mediterranean area and the Caucasus. Elsewhere, too, in the United States for instance, more or less similar behaviour can be found. On the basis of detailed social and psychological research, it has been established that men from the southern states of the United States are more easily offended, respond more quickly to an insult and that the environment more readily accepts a violent response.[23]

Here is a relation with Hofstede's masculinity and collectivism dimensions that were mentioned earlier in this chapter.[24] In a society where men have a cultural position of their own, aimed at competition and dominance, hurting a man's pride is more likely to occur and the risk of violence is greater. Especially when reputation matters are involved — an indication of collectivism — this type of reaction is more likely to occur. Other research has shown that this pattern evolves as a consequence of the way in which children, especially boys, are socialised. If they are socialised for aggression in their late childhood, this is the strongest predictor of homicide and assault at the societal level.[25]

This culture-bound phenomenon can also be recognised in more large-scale violence occurring during civil wars and uprisings. In the Balkans, there has always been a tradition of honour crimes, feuds and vendettas. Also, in Chechnya, there is the age-old heroic mythology of 'blood feuds' and ancestral customs, which plays an important 'motivating' role in the war against the Russians. As a result, Chechen youngsters are easily incited to violence. A quarrel among Chechens themselves could lead to prolonged bloodshed, but the hatred of Russians runs even deeper as almost every Chechen has lost at least one member of the family in the protracted conflict. Therefore, the Chechens will not stop their honour feud until the last Russian soldier has disappeared from their country.[26] Chechen patience, where blood feud is concerned, is legendary. In Moscow, which is a regular target for Chechen attacks and kidnappings, the inhabitants will know all about this by now.

Notes

1. Huntington, S.P., *The Clash of Civilisations and the Remaking of the World Order*, Simon and Schuster, New York, 2003 (first print 1996). See also Harrison L.E. and Huntington S.P. (eds.), *Culture Matters. How Values Shape Human Progress*, Basic Books, New York, 2000; Berger, P.L. and Huntington S.P. (eds.), *Many Globalizations. Cultural Diversity in the Contemporary World*, Oxford University Press, Oxford, 2002.

2. Hofstede, G.H., *Cultures and Organizations. Sotfware of the Mind*, McGraw-Hill, London, 1991; Hofstede, G.H., *Culture's Consequences. Comparing Values, Behaviors, Institutions and Organizations Across Nations*, Thousand Oaks, Sage, 2001; see also Vinken, H., Soeters J. and Ester P. (eds.), *Comparing Cultures. Dimensions of Culture in a Comparative Perspective*, Brill, Leiden, 2004.

3. Inglehart R. and Baker, W.E., Modernization, cultural change, and the persistence of traditional values, *American Sociological Review*, 65, 19–51, 2000. See also Vinken H., *et al.* (eds.), op. cit., 2004.

4. Hofstede, G.H., op. cit., 96–101, 1991.

5. van de Vliert E. *et al.*, Temperature, cultural masculinity, and domestic political violence, *Journal of Cross-Cultural Psychology*, 1999 (30), 291–314.

6. Hofstede, G.H., op. cit., 100–101, 1991.

7. Hofstede, G.H., op. cit., Chapter 5, especially pages 126–130, 1991.

8. Anonymous, *Griekenland pakt racisme hard aan* (Greece comes down heavily on racism), *Volkskrant*, 13 November 2003.

9. Hofstede, G.H., op. cit., Chapters 4 and 6, 2001.

10. See also Triandis, H., *Individualism and Collectivism*, Westview Press, Boulder, 1995. This author speaks about 'tight' (collectivistic) and 'loose' (individualistic) societies; in 'tight' societies, the probability of intergroup conflict is higher.

11. Hofstede, G.H., Images of Europe, *Netherlands' Journal of Social Sciences*, 30, 63–82, 1994. See also Hofstede, op. cit., Chapters 3, 4, 5 and 6, 2001.

12. Tomasic, D., The structure of Balkan society, *American Journal of Sociology*, 52, 132–133, 1946; van de Port, M., op. cit., 1994 provides similar descriptions. The 'demand' of the Croatian government to get an 'all-white' UN Peace Force and the fact that non-white UN military in Croatia regularly became victims of racism underline this cultural profile once again. See Anonymous, *Kroatië stuurt aan op 'blanke' VN-vredesmacht* (Croatia aims for 'white' UN Peace Force), *Volkskrant*, 11 April 1995. About Rwanda it has been observed that conformity is very deep, highly developed and that everyone obeys authority. This is a clear signal of a large degree of power distance in that country; see Gourevitch, Ph., op. cit., 23, 1998.

13. Hofstede, G.H., op. cit., 1994; for a precise comparison with Belgium, see Soeters, J., Culture and conflict: an application of Hofstede's theory to the conflict in the former Yugoslavia, *Peace and Conflict. Journal of Peace Psychology*, 2, 233–244, 1996. See also Soeters, J., Governmental and administrative cultures in Belgium and the Netherlands: from divergence to convergence?, *International Review of Administrative Sciences*, 61, 265–278, 1995.

14. Hofstede, G.H., op. cit., 1994.

15. Hofstede, G.H., op. cit., 1994.
16. Hofstede, G.H., op. cit., 2001; Vinken, H., Soeters J. and Ester P. (eds.), op. cit., 2004; Inglehart R. and Baker, W.E., op. cit., 2000.
17. Huntington, S.P., op. cit., 81–101, 2003 (first print 1996). On glocalisation, Meyer, J.W., Globalization. Sources and effects on national states and societies, *International Sociology*, 15, 233–248, 2000. The example referring to Ankara is in Helvacioglu, B., Globalization in the neighbourhood: from the nation state to Bilkent Center, *International Sociology*, 15, 326–342, 2000.
18. Voorhoeve, J.J.C., *Peace, Profits and Principles. A Study of Dutch Foreign Policy*, Martinus Nijhoff, The Hague, 1979.
19. Broch-Due (ed.), V., op. cit, Routledge, London and New York, 25, 2005.
20. Franke, H., op. cit., 41–42, 1991; Leistra G. and Nieuwbeerta, P., op. cit., 2003.
21. Leistra G. and Nieuwbeerta, P., op. cit., 2003.
22. Nisbett R.E. and Cohen, D., *Culture of Honor. The Psychology of Violence in the South*, Westview Press, Boulder, 1996; Cohen D. *et al.*, Insult, aggression, and the Southern culture of honor: an "experimental" ethnography, *Journal of Personality and Social Psychology*, 70, 945–960, 1996; Cohen, D., Law, social policy, and violence: the impact of regional cultures, *Journal of Personality and Social Psychology*, 70, 961–978, 1996.
23. Nisbett R.E. and Cohen, D., op. cit., 1996; Cohen, D., op. cit., 1996.
24. Japan is an interesting exception in this connection. It is a country with a very high degree of masculinity (and an average degree of collectivism), but the number of murders and homicides in that country is surprisingly small.
25. Ember C.R. and Ember, M., War, socialization, and interpersonal violence, *Journal of Conflict Resolution*, 38, 620–646, 1994.
26. Winslow D. and Moelker, R., op. cit., 2002; Tishkov, V., op. cit., 99, 2004. For these phenomena in the Balkans, see Wheatcroft, A., op. cit., 248, 2004.

6

RATIONALISATION OF EVIL

In 1963, the former Nazi Adolf Eichmann was condemned in Jerusalem for committing crimes against humanity. Several authors have reported this protracted trial. Hannah Arendts' report is possibly the most authoritative, as she makes apt observations on the circumstances in which these war crimes could occur.[1] Her characterisation of these circumstances as the 'banality of evil' points at a long-term process related to violence. Although this aspect of violence and conflict does not have any direct bearing on the internal conflicts that are the focus of the present analysis, it is nevertheless too important to be ignored. Besides, it will soon become clear that this matter, so closely associated with the practices of World War II, is also of importance, albeit indirectly, in understanding the atrocities in the former Yugoslavia, Rwanda, Sierra Leone and so many other places in the world. Certain aspects of the recent terrorist attacks too can be explained by means of the analysis below.

It comes down to the observation that in modern, bureaucratic societies, conditions have emerged that strip violence of its moral dimensions. The differentiated and technological character of modern society implies the severing of rationality from ethical considerations. The bureaucratic organisation is the product of the development of centuries directed at the rationalisation of managerial processes. In the process, the ethical dimension has gradually been sidelined. According to the famous study by sociologist Zygmunt Bauman, the Holocaust was possible because of the fact that not a single individual needed to feel personally responsible for the crimes against the Jews. The hunting down of Jews in the various countries, the transportation to the concentration camps and even the acts in the camps were organised in such a labour-divisional and rational manner that moral judgement was not 'required'. All acts were methodically sound, procedural, technical and impersonal. The bureaucratic system manipulated the people into contributing to the realisation of the most horrific deeds. Quoting from Bauman, 'If Midas's touch transformed everything into gold, SS administration transformed everything which has come into its orbit — including its victims — into an integral part of the chain of command, an area subject to the strictly disciplinary rules, and freed from moral judgement.' and, 'The technical-administrative success of the Holocaust was due in part to the skilful utilisation of "moral sleeping pills" made available by modern bureaucracy and modern technology.'[2]

This can be illustrated by the following. In the persecution of the Dutch Jews, the municipal civil servants were involved in passing on the names and addresses of future victims, police officers in picking them up from their homes, railway personnel in transporting them, and finally traders (bakers, etc.) in providing them with food in the transition camps. In short, the whole process involved many straight-laced Dutch citizens, each of whom made a tiny contribution; and they only did this because they were told to do so by their superiors or clients. This explains why, in a moral sense, they did not feel responsible at all, or only to a very limited extent, for their part in this genocide. This is what Bauman's thesis boils down to.

Due to the ever-extending labour-divisional and rational character of modern society, the genocide could happen in a 'compartmentalised' manner, i.e. separate from normal society. The word 'separate' should be given broad scope in this context. It has a psychological meaning (delivering names or bread was only a small part of one's normal work) as well as a social aspect (only a few professional groups were involved). In addition, there is a spatial side to it (the camps were in remote locations) as well as a time-related one (the work was done outside normal hours, mostly at night or in the early morning). This is why these 'dyscivilisation' processes (i.e. the total breakdown of civilised behaviour) can occur in modern 'civilised' societies, even while these civilisations keep on functioning in the meantime.[3]

More precisely, moral objections against the execution of violence can be eroded by at least three factors, two of which belong to the standard elements of a bureaucracy — authorisation and routinisation. Dehumanisation is the third.[4]

Authorisation takes place when superiors order their subordinates to use violence. Stanley Milgram's widely known experiments speak volumes in this respect.[5] They showed that normal people were prepared to inflict serious pain and injury on others. In the experiments, this was done by administering ostensible electric shocks to subjects. People do this only because they are ordered by an authority, a superior to do so; in this case, it was the white-coated leader of the experiment. Apparently, an order from a superior provides enough excuse for the possible reprehensibility of their acts. A thorough sociological study into the functioning of the notorious concentration camps in Nazi Germany revealed that it was not at all necessary to have sadists, criminals or fanatics to do the 'dirty job'. Provided there was enough intimidation and pressure from above, ordinary people (book-keepers, civil servants, doctors, waitresses and female industrial labourers) lent themselves eminently well for the most lugubrious tasks in the camps. Especially when those at the top 'guarantee' that one can save one's own skin, people are inclined to obey the more powerful in their environment.[6] This is what has been called the 'dark side of obedience', which comes along with the inability to think and a lack of compassion and caring.[7]

Routinisation pre-eminently refers to bureaucracy and in particular, to formal rules, exact task and role descriptions, formal-legal issue of orders and a labour-divisional organisation in which most single workers do not see the 'final product'. In routinised systems, the workers simply do their task. Often, there is no, or only limited, contact with the victims, which minimalises the possibility of personal sympathy. This latter point is also recognisable in the striving of the military for 'violence at a distance', preferably from an aircraft.

Dehumanisation, finally refers to the consequences of stereotyping and ideological indoctrination. Crimes and violence committed against representatives of certain groups are not morally 'objectionable' and are legitimised by the organisation, since these groups are considered inferior anyway and as not belonging to the human species. In the next chapter, we will come back to this factor. A horrifying combination of routinisation and dehuminisation is the way the Rwandase murderers considered the killing, as 'a job that needed to be done', comparable to the heavy 'chopping' and 'hacking' they were used to doing in the plantations.[8]

The above analysis, indicated by de Swaan as the 'bureaucratisation of barbarism'[9], is directed at explaining the Holocaust. But it is fascinating to see the parallels with the preparation and execution of recent terrorist attacks (9/11, Bali, Istanbul, Madrid). The arrests made afterwards often reveal that scores of people were involved. There are those who take care of the banking affairs, others provide the passports, yet others make the route descriptions. Some provide the vehicles, others deliver the materials for the bombs and there are the bomb engineers who actually make the bombs; and on top are the organisers (personnel, finances) and directors who define the targets. All the people involved, with the exception of those who actually carry out the attack, have only a small part in the final result. But their involvement began through the processes that we have seen above — authorisation, routinisation and dehumanisation of those who deserve to be punished (Westeners, Americans, Britons and Jews).

Discussion
Holocaust: bureaucratic system or German anti-semitism?[10]

In 1996, Harvard political scientist Daniel Goldhagen caused a stir with the publication of his book Hitler's Willing Executioners: Ordinary Germans and the Holocaust. *In this doctoral thesis, he describes how ordinary Germans co-operated voluntarily, consciously*

and with full conviction in the persecution of the Jews. He is quite definite about the guilt of the Germans. In a newspaper interview, he is crystal clear, 'It can be said about the Germans — without Germans no holocaust. This cannot be said about any other nation. Should we really argue about whether the holocaust originated in Germany?'

In his argument, he opposes the view of the holocaust as an impersonal process of almost industrial mass destruction. He lays the full blame of all this with the German people. This accusation puts him in a tradition of authors who have tried to explain the holocaust from typical German cultural characteristics. Norbert Elias in his Studien über die Deutschen *pointed at the relatively violent and antagonistic character of German civilisation (masculinity!). Arguing Hofstede's line of thinking, it is especially the combination with uncertainty avoidance (what is foreign is dangerous) that is striking. This attitude can also be recognised in the various Berufsverbote that the German authorities imposed on people who wanted to become civil servants, but who were considered to be too left (the seventies) or too sectarian (Scientology Church, 1997).*

But the question remains whether this explains everything there is to the holocaust. Goldhagen fails to make sufficiently clear which Germans were perpetrators and which were not. Besides, the position of non-German perpetrators — and they were plentiful, including many Dutchmen — remains unclear. Finally, the massacre in the former Soviet Union, under Stalin, of millions of citizens cannot be explained very well by referring to German culture. In short, there seems to be more to explaining the holocaust (and other cases of genocide) than solely the German culture perspective.

Perhaps there are also matters that relate to the manipulative bureaucratic system that incorporates the 'banality of evil'.

Relation with (a lack of) discipline

The relevance of the Holocaust analysis goes further, though. The first two points, i.e. authorisation and routinisation, are also extremely relevant for the modern 'violence organisations', such as the armed forces and the police. A key theme in connection with this is discipline, i.e. 'obedience' to the organisation regime. In the control of violence, discipline is a very positive quality. It is an expression of the professionalisation of the military organisation and as such, it can be considered an element of the civilisation tendency discussed before.[11] Discipline is an important factor in the prevention and containment of violence and conflict.

It is not a coincidence that the various internal conflicts all over the world are characterised by a great measure of lawlessness and lack of discipline.

Violence in Rwanda, Somalia, Chechnya or Bosnia has been, first and foremost, decentralised violence, which is not under the permanent supervision of a central leadership. It is often the work of relatively independently operating, mutinying and raping militias of marginal (wo)men, who know no discipline or fighting codes. A spectacular example of this is the so-called child soldiers, who play an important part in the various African conflicts. These children — both boys and girls — varying in age between eight and fourteen, are usually both victim and perpetrator at the same time. They are victims because they have often lost their families, been raped themselves and have no roof over their heads, a position that forces them to join the gangs. They are also sometimes perpetrators as they volunteer for revenge actions and the 'wargame'. What moves the boys to join these quasi-military gangs is not so difficult to understand. For girls and young women, the motivation to join is basically the same. Additionally, the girls' motives can be found in a desire to follow their 'sweethearts' and besides that, some girls think the uniform is rather cool. These groups of child soldiers usually operate without specific orders or supervision, often even without any radio contact with the higher echelon. They determine their own 'rules of the game' with regard to the use of violence and they kill easily and mercilessly; ambushing is their favourite 'pastime'.[12] Although child soldiers are predominantly an African phenomenon, they definitely occur elsewhere on the globe. In the very first days of 2005, the Liberation Tamil Tigers in Sri Lanka started to crimp young orphans who had lost their parents in the Tsunami flooding only a week earlier.[13]

The police actions of the Netherlands in the Dutch East Indies provide another example of a lapse into violence as a result of failing discipline. During those actions, there were serious acts of violence on both sides by relatively independently operating units — mob-like gangs on the rebel side and covertly operating special units of the Dutch army. The excesses of violence did not seem to differ much for the rebel forces and Dutch troops as far as their structure and functioning was concerned.[14]

Discipline, as an expression of a centralised organisation, limits disorderly violence and as such carries a lot of good in it, but it also has its dangers. In a disciplined combat organisation, orders issued in a widely branched chain of command have to outweigh the individual, personal opinions and preferences of the personnel. In the ideal situation, from the point of view of the organisation, the worker is dependent on the organisation and sacrifices his own moral convictions in order to realise the objectives of the organisation. The socialisation regime of many organisations is directed at attaining this situation. It is the intention, implicit or explicit, that the subordinates begin to see the orders as inevitable task obligations, without experiencing any personal responsibility for their actions. In such cases, the organisation strives for an attitude among its personnel that will lead to a 'slavish overattention to orders'.[15]

Insofar as there are any moral questions in such an organisation at all, they are a matter for the higher echelons. The violence that emerges in such an organisational context is organised effectively and rationally and in many respects superior to the bloody orgies that characterise the uncontrolled violence of the present day conflicts. But by centralising the authority to a few at the top, this disciplined, bureaucratised violence can degenerate into inhuman behaviour. World War II and the Vietnam War (endless carpet bombing) have sufficiently proven this point. The result is 'crimes of obedience' (My Lai).[16]

From an organisation-sociological viewpoint, acts of violence originate from two extreme situations, as is shown in Figure 6.

In opposition to the irregular, undisciplined and independent violence stands the rationalised evil that can occur in the centralised, bureaucratised violence organisations. However, the situation is not always so clear. Sometimes, violence evolves in an atmosphere of centralised violence-inducing policies eliciting undisciplined behaviour. The aforementioned specialised Dutch military units sometimes really ran 'wild' during the police actions in Indonesia, leading to what has been called the 'derailment of violence'. But this happened against the background of top commanders condoning this behaviour because it proved effective in the fight against the revolutionaries. In much the same way, the tortures at the Abu Ghraib prison in Baghdad by the United States military seems to have been the consequence of 'some kids getting out of control'. On the other hand, special military intelligence policies, intended to generate information about the growing insurgence in Iraq, led the guards to believe that more or less everything was allowed, if only it produced information on future threats. Hence, a grey zone developed in which physical coercion and sexual humiliation of prisoners were deemed legitimate.[17]

Apart from the centralisation of policies and activities (or the lack thereof), there is something else of importance in connection with this, viz. the 'fear' factor. The primal emotion of fear is a theme that has been paid too little attention to in the social sciences; erroneously, for fear is an important motive underlying many human actions. This point is also relevant when studying the 'banality of evil', as it is possible to hypothesise

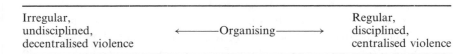

| Irregular, undisciplined, decentralised violence | ←——————Organising——————→ | Regular, disciplined, centralised violence |

Figure 6 Organisation and execution of violence.

that the disciplined violence on the right side of Figure 6, in particular, is inspired by fear. Not only the fear of losing one's life, as in the concentration camps, but also the fear of missing out on promotions and losing the favour of one's superiors, as in violence organisations. Or even, the fear of having to face (military) justice and thus run the danger of being excluded. Loyalty to the bureaucratic system, in short, is often inspired by the fear of losing the protection of that very system.[18]

On the left side of the figure, with reference to the irregular and uncontrolled violence, it is precisely the absence of fear that forms the background to the violence. In the absence of any superiors to supervise, one is out of sight and besides, there is no system to fit in, anyway. Further, in the case of the present day conflicts and attacks, the worst atrocities are committed by unhinged juveniles, who know no fear of loss of work or — for instance, as is the case with the AIDS-infected Hutu youths — life. Often drugs (crack, amphetamines and local concoctions) play a part in repressing the fear of combat. For girls, however, fear does play a part; they are raped if they do not perform well in battle, and if they do, they are raped anyway.[19] In any case, fear and its absence thereof can both lead to violence, though of different types.

In the bureaucratic violence organisation, the leadership is responsible for the result of the functioning of the organisation. The bureaucratic organisation, as a vehicle of modernisation and rationalisation, is rigged with a 'big brother' culture, strongly developed control technologies and a far advanced command structure. There are sufficient indications that this type of organising is becoming increasingly dominant in the world.[20]

For the leadership of such violence organisations, the armed forces in particular, the threat of a separation between ethics and rationality is all the more important, as generating combat power is one of the ultimate goals. It lays a heavy burden on the moral insight of the leadership in modernised violence organisations. This moral understanding will develop better when military decisions are more transparent and allow better control by politicians, the media and military personnel. After all, it is precisely the organisations that employ methods which avoid the scrutiny of outsiders and insiders alike that run the biggest risk of developing in a harmful direction. The primacy of politics and the controlling function of the media are becoming increasingly critical factors in decisions concerning life or death, and that is what they should be. Influences from society, politics and the media can foster a multiple discretional perspective in military decision makers, allowing them to come to balanced decisions.[21] Apart from this, it is important that personnel of all ranks are not only, or not so much, trained in obedience and discipline, but also, or in particular, in the development of personal responsibility and discretion. This moral obligation should include the ability and courage to object, if necessary.[22]

Notes

1. Arendt, H., *Eichmann in Jerusalem: a Report on the Banality of Evil*, Faber and Faber, London, 1963.
2. Bauman, Z., *Modernity and the Holocaust*, Polity Press, Cambridge, 1991. The quotes are on pages 22 and 26. See also St. Mennell, op. cit., 274, 1992; Collins, R., op. cit., 432–434, 1974.
3. de Swaan, A., *Dyscivilisatie, massale uitroeiing, en de staat* (Dyscivilisation, mass extermination, and the state), *Amsterdams Sociologisch Tijdschrift*, 26, 289–301, 1999.
4. Kelman, H.C., Violence without moral constraint, *Journal of Social Issues*, 29, 29–61, 1973.
5. Milgram, St., Behavior study of obedience, *Journal of Abnormal and Social Psychology*, 67, 371–378, 1963.
6. Sofsky, Z., *Die Ordnung des Terrors: das Konzentrationslager (The Order of Terror; the Concentration Camp)*, Fischer, Frankfurt am Main, 317, 1993. See also Lammers, C.J., The organization of mass murder, *Organization Studies*, 16, 139–156, 1995.
7. Verweij, D., The dark side of obedience: the consequences of Hannah Arendt's analysis of the Eichmann case, *Professional Ethics*, 10, 143–158, 2002.
8. Hatzfeld, J., op. cit., 2003.
9. de Swaan, A., op. cit., 293, 1999.
10. In this discussion, the following sources have been used: Goldhagen, D., *Hitler's Willing Executioners: Ordinary Germans and the Holocaust*, Knopf, New York, 1996; Elias, N., *Studien über die Deutschen (Studies on the Germans)*, Suhrkamp, Frankfurt am Main, 1989; Hofstede, G.H., op. cit., 1991; Muskens, G., *Hitler's gewillige beulen* (Hitler's willing executioners), Facta, 4–8, especially pages 8–9, 1996.
11. Teitler, G., op. cit., Chapter 1, 1972.
12. Peters K. and Richards, P., 'Why we fight': voices of youth combatants in Sierra Leone, *Africa*, 68, 183–210, 1998. For undisciplined violent behaviour in Chechnya, see Tishkov, V., op. cit., 65, 2004.
13. Kranenberg, A., *Jachtseizoen van de Tamil Tijgers is geopend* (The hunting season of the Tamil Tigers is open), *Volkskrant*, 7 January 2005.
14. van Doorn J.A.A. and Hendrix, W.J., op. cit., 135 and 168, 1970.
15. Lee Hamilton V. and Sanders, J., Responsibility and risk in organizational crimes of obedience, in Staw B.M. and Cummings L.L. (eds.), *Research in Organizational Behavior*, JAI Press, Greenwich, 49–90, 1992.
16. Kelman H.C. and Lee Hamilton, V., *Crimes of Obedience. Toward a Social Psychology of Authority and Responsibility*, Yale UP, New Haven and London, 1989. See also Walzer, M., op. cit., 1992.
17. Hersh, S.M., Torture at Abu Ghraib, *The New Yorker*, 10 May 2004; Hersh, S.M., The gray zone, *The New Yorker*, 24 May 2004. See also Hersh, S.M., *Chain of Command*, HarperCollins, New York, 2004.
18. Flam, H., Fear, loyalty and greedy organizations, in Fineman, St., (ed.), *Emotion in Organizations*, Sage, London, 58–75, 1994.
19. Peters K. and Richards, P., op. cit., 187–187 and 190–192, 1998.

20. Ritzer, G., *The McDonaldization of Society*, Pine Forge Press, Thousand Oaks, 1993.
21. An analysis of so-called harmful organisations can be found in Masuch, M., The determinants of organizational harm, *Research in the Sociology of Organizations*, 9, 79–102, 1991.
22. Lee Hamilton V. and Sanders, J., op. cit., 80–84, 1992; Verweij, D. op. cit., 2002.

Part II

MICRO AND SHORT-TERM FACTORS

7

GROUP BINDING, STEREOTYPING AND IDEOLOGISING

With the fifth factor, violence as a consequence of the rationalisation of evil, the exploration of the breeding ground of violence and conflict is complete and with it, the macro-conditions for a greater or lesser chance of an outbreak of violence and conflict have been defined. But the concrete behaviour of the people who cause the actual violence has still remained unexplored. These micro-processes will be dealt with below, beginning with the dynamics of group binding, stereotyping and ideologising. It must, however, be stressed that macro- and micro-processes are closely related and can sometimes hardly be distinguished.

People distinguish themselves through the groups they belong to, or consider themselves to belong to. This was already clear in the treatment of the group–grid model and the discussion of the 'individualism-collectivism' culture dimension. When there are clearly discernible boundaries between groups of people, it can be said that there is clear group binding. The phenomenon contains a subjective perception component in that a strong group binding implies an explicit antithesis between 'us' and 'them'. In this context, the concept of 'stereotyping' is of importance.[1]

Stereotypes are socially constructed images; they are fixed, if not rooted ideas of members of one group about the members, i.e. all members, of another group. Here, the four 'Rs' mentioned earlier (race, religion, region and record) form the pretext for group distinction and the stereotypes. Especially their visible expressions (skin colour, head dress, outward appearance, etc.) play an important signalling role in this process. But also less discernible aspects, such as accent, language and dialect, names and eating habits, are important in this context.[2] In the Netherlands, someone with a Southern (Limburg) accent is still often considered to be less educated, not to be taken quite seriously and sometimes, not to be trusted. These stereotypes still harbour century-old prejudices connected with religion in general (Protestantism versus Catholicism) and subjection in particular (Protestant authorities occupying the Southern Catholic regions in former times).

In the conflicts in Rwanda, Burundi and the Congo, stereotypes about the Hutus and Tutsis played an important part. Tutsis were always considered to be tall, physical, handsome, proud and intelligent people with leadership capabilities, while the Hutus were seen as scarcely more than losers, peasants and slaves. These ideas are based on a range of perceptions and misconceptions and half-truths that have existed for centuries and have taken root in the views of Westerners about these countries. In particular, yesterday's colonisers have made an unmistakable contribution in this respect. For the Belgian colonisers, who were following the ideas of German scientists, the Tutsis were superior to the other communities; they were the 'Europeans with a black skin'. The distinction between Hutus and Tutsis became official when the Belgian authorities began to establish municipal registers in 1926, with an entry of every citizen's ethnic origin. Partly because of this formal government policy these stereotypes have also nestled in the mutual perceptions of the communities in the country itself. They are stereotypes that still lead a vital and sometimes fatal existence, even decades after the Europeans have left.[3]

Incidentally, this phenomenon is more widespread than the Belgian heritage in Rwanda and Burundi. In practically every colonisation process, European authorities — the Dutch, British, French and German — developed their stereotypical preference or disapproval of certain communities. Representatives of these preferred communities were then given positions of authority in order to function as 'agents' of the colonial rulers. Usually this policy of 'ethnic nepotism' was employed in order to be able to carry out a divide-and-rule strategy. In the context of the increasing tension between Muslims and the West since 9/11, it is interesting to note how the British, in their colonial days, denigrated and ridiculed Islamic leaders in a stereotypical manner. Epithets such as 'Mad Mullah' were quite common and the highest Islamic titles of 'caliph' and 'khansama' were used to indicate the most subordinate functions in British colonial government.[4]

Clash of stereotypes[5]

The current tensions between the Western (Christian) and the Muslim worlds date back centuries. During the Crusades and the Reconquista wars in Spain, each side used images of the other party as being infidel, i.e. not adhering to true religion, cruel, degraded, dangerous, savage, barbarous, violent, unclean as well as morally defective. Even sexual manners, especially of the women ('lustful'), were stereotyped back and forth. Those images stem from eras when the two sides were really at war with each other. Nowadays, there is no longer such hostility, although Muslims all over the world may perceive the current Western military presence in Iraq as such.

Today's stereotypes are clearly less aggressive, because in general, the tensions are less and the interdependence is far more developed. However, the events of 9/11 have uncovered a new increase of mutual stereotyping, making political Muslims believe that (all) Westerners are soulless, decadent, money grabbing, faithless, arrogant, frivolous and greedy. At the same time, quite some Westerners are inclined to think that (all) Muslims are cruel, passive, discriminating of women and in general, lagging behind.

What are the more precise characteristics of stereotypes? First of all, they serve a purpose. They have a stratifying, distinguishing significance. In itself that is an important and useful function for human beings, as it makes life more structured. For this very good reason, stereotyping is also known as a 'mental efficiency tool'. But there are some flaws attached to this 'efficient' ordering. On the one hand, it is not certain that the characteristics attributed to a certain group are in line with (objective) reality. Is it really true that the members of group B are 'lazier' or 'more stupid' than those of group A? Often stereotyping is about group labels with an appreciating or depreciating character, the truth of which is very hard to ascertain anyway. Stereotypical judgements very easily become prejudices. But, on the other hand, it is unlikely that these group labels, even if they were correct, would be applicable, without exception, to every individual member of the group for which the stereotyping is supposed to be relevant. Characterisations of groups are at best right an average, i.e. there is always a distribution around the statistical mean and therefore, there will always be individual exceptions to the 'rule'.

Secondly, stereotypes are applicable to groups with a social identity. But at the same time, they are used by groups with a social identity. Stereotypes are shared cultural meanings or common pictures of the mind that give a subjective feeling of common origin. Own group stereotypes (*autostereotypes*) refer to characteristics of which every group member can be proud; they are characteristics which enable him to feel superior with regard to the other group. The stereotypes about the other group (*heterostereotypes*), on the other hand, always contain negative connotations. This positive or negative appreciation exists even when the behaviour is exactly the same, which implies that the others just cannot do things right. Drunkenness makes a 'real man' of a member of one's own group, and a member of the outgroup an 'alcoholic'. Or in sociologist Robert Merton's famous words, 'ingroup virtues are outgroup vices'; the virtues of one's own people are the shortcomings of the others.[6] Besides, own group perceptions offer enough room for nuance and individual variation. The perceptions of the outgroup, on the other hand, do not distinguish between individuals.

There is also a third point of importance. Stereotypes have a self-assuring or self-refuting effect. This has to do with one of the basic rules in sociology, the so-called Thomas theorem: 'If men define situations as real, these situations are real in their consequences.' In other words, if people have ideas and expectations about something, then these ideas and expectations have consequences for what is actually going to happen next. Examples of this are numerous. As seen above, when the Europeans were in power in Rwanda and Burundi, they were convinced that the Tutsis were more intelligent and 'more European' than the other communities in these areas. This is why they thought the Tutsis were more suitable for taking up positions of authority in the colony. On the basis of this idea, they offered them more educational opportunities and higher positions as compared to the members of other communities. As a result, the Tutsis were indeed better equipped to function according to the wishes of their European masters and in this way, 'Tutsification' of the colonial government became a fact. This happened especially in the 1930s. This is a clear case of a self-fulfilling prophesy. Another example of the Thomas rule is when a party expects an attack from another party, the former will arm itself, with the result that the latter is afraid of attacking it. This is an example of a self-refuting expectation. Whether self-assuring or self-refuting, stereotypes create their own dynamics and turn present expectations and ideas into future realities.[7]

From stereotype to ideology

Generally speaking, stereotypes are firmly rooted — they hardly change and cannot be changed. They are acquired during childhood, even before a person has a clear perception of the group to which the stereotype is supposed to apply. All this is not so bad, for in normal circumstances, stereotypes do not cause many problems.

However, the phenomenon becomes more extreme and intense in times of social tension, animosity and danger. This is particularly the case when one's livelihood, such as land, water, housing and jobs, become scarce. Then, there is a collective fear of the future and the tension between groups rises. Group boundaries become more visible, group identities become clearer and rivalry between groups grows. In case of tension and crisis, the group binding, or the cohesion inside the group grows. So, in times of crisis, the individual person rallies safely behind the identity of the group. But this increased cohesion within the group is in direct relation to the growing sense of animosity between the groups. In this light, it is not surprising that the survey in the former Yugoslavia mentioned earlier, revealed that a rise in unemployment was coupled with a relatively high measure of intolerance towards persons from a different community.[8]

Especially when people feel their livelihood is threatened and experience the proximity of death, a process of negative stereotyping and a boosting of the group feeling begin. The reaction of the American people to the attacks on the Twin Towers is an example of this. Immediately afterwards, there was a surge of patriotism, as was manifest from the little flags on virtually every car. At the same time, an enmity towards everything with even the slightest whiff of Arabic origin began to emerge in the whole country. The large support of the American population for the military actions in Afghanistan and Iraq in 2002 and 2003 must also be seen in this light.[9]

When rivalry increases, the stereotypes are used more frequently and they can eventually lead to ideologies — social and political expressions of a reality perceived as well as aspired for by a particular group. So, ideology is interpretation and ambition both rolled in one. It can take on various guises. Thus, its background can be socio-economic (capitalism, Marxism), religious (Christianity, Islam), or ethnic ('Native country back!', 'Own people first!', 'A state of our own!'). Ideologies vary from Marx to Mohammed, as is sometimes said.

Often this political or group ideology is employed to accuse another group of having caused disasters, such as economic decline. This accusation, then, provides the excuse to undertake certain violent actions against these groups, such as orchestrated or spontaneous harassment, attacks or terrorist actions. The other, supposedly hostile, group is called all the worst names. Thus, in Bosnia, the Muslims were repeatedly called 'Turks', a reference to the former Ottoman Empire. In Russia, people from the Caucasus, Chechnya in particular, are consistently referred to as 'blacks', a term that is not intended as flattery. But the treatment can be much more negative. Members of the opposite party may be called everything that is inhuman. In the previous chapter, the term dehumanisation was mentioned. In the Sudan, the communities from the South are called 'slaves' and 'animals' respectively, taking away all psychological inhibitions against killing. In the Rwandan conflict, the hostile feelings towards the Tutsis were systematically stirred up in the media by calling them treacherous, unreliable and even devilish — with horns, hoofs, tails and all. The culmination of the dehumanisation of the Tutsis was the epithet *injenzi* (cockroaches). What had to be done with them was clear — this pernicious vermin could only be trampled upon or beaten to death.[10]

Eventually, this may lead to pure hostility as a political ideology and the consequences may be open violence, murder, ethnic cleansing and deportation of the hated community. Incidentally, enmity is just as often, if not more, directed at groups of equal status as it is at higher ranking groups. Respect and fear of the social elite often prevent frustrations from becoming open enmity against these superior groups.[11]

World history is rife with examples of the above-mentioned mechanisms. They range from the many acts of violence in the name of Christianity and Islam against heathens and infidels, the Nazi ideology against the Jews and the ideas of colonial powers about 'natives', 'extremists' and 'slaves' ('apes'), to the attacks and deportations committed in the name of something or somebody and the mutual typifications and ensuing ideologies of Serbs,

Muslims and Croats. Ugresic's book on the former Yugoslavia abounds with them; these 'perceptions' are acquired in earliest childhood and therefore last for generations.[12]

In a more abstract sense, these processes can be analysed in terms of identification and dysidentification. We live in a time in which the 'power of identity'[13] is dominant and processes like identification and dysidentification are extremely important in many situations. Identification is the emotional pendant of group formation; people identify with, feel one with, the members of their own group. Dysidentification is the instinctive expression of the exclusion of others, the people of the outgroup, those whom one is not allowed to pity. Identification and dysidentification are not opposites; in fact, as shown in Figure 7, they belong together as the sides of a triangle, the base of which is formed by ignorance and indifference ('other people simply do not interest me, I know nothing').

The greater the identification with members of one's own group, the higher the extent of instinctive exclusion of others (dysidentification). Analogous to outgroup vices and ingroup virtues, negative qualities (lust for violence, unreasonableness) of one's own group are denied, and attributed to the group that one instinctively distances oneself from ('We do not mean any harm, they do'). All in all, both processes — identification and

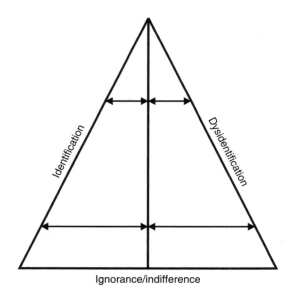

Ignorance/indifference

Figure 7 Identification and dysidentification as sides of an emotional triangle. Source: Based on de Swaan, A. *Uitdijende kringen van desidentificatie: gedachten over Rwanda* (Widening circles of dysidentification: reflections on Rwanda), *Amsterdams Sociologisch Tijdschrift*, 24, 3–23, 1997.

dysidentification — run parallel with each other and are closely related. One does not happen without the other; the stronger the one, the stronger the other. In de Swaan's words, 'the us-er, the them-er'. The implication of this reasoning is that to prevent violence and conflict, it is better for a population to be closer to the base of the triangle. On the other hand, indifference can make people close their eyes to acts of violence that take place in their proximity; a phenomenon that happens regularly in the individualised Western societies, as was seen in Chapter 2.[14]

Manipulation, opportunism and dynamics

It is important to realise that during the phase of (political) struggle these processes of identification and dysidentification often have a highly manipulative, opportunistic and dynamic character. Anthropologists like Frederick Barth have pointed out that groups and their ensuing collective identities are not a natural phenomenon, but are quite emphatically social constructs. The political elite (chiefs, political entrepreneurs, brokers) play an important 'entrepreneurial' role in this.[15]

Most of the above-mentioned processes begin with a small group of people whose success is primarily dependent on the size of the network they can activate to support their mission. Especially financial support and the support with regard to gaining access to the positions of power in society (public administration, police and army, possibly the business world, but first and foremost, the media) is important. Political entrepreneurs will go out of their way to appropriate existing organisations that will help them to seize more power. The size of the network and the selectivity with which the political entrepreneurs choose participants, in particular, is an important contributory factor in the success of their 'political enterprise'.[16]

Apart from this, the success of their 'political enterprise' is dependent on the extent to which they are capable of conducting 'symbolic management'. Many symbols and rituals are products of conscious attempts at giving people a sense of identity and continuity. In this way, the 'political entrepreneurs' create new myths or revive old ones. According to the late Chechen leader Dudayev, Islam must have emerged, not in the lifeless desert of Arabia among nomadic tribes, but in the earthly paradise among peoples of high culture and mutual respect, i.e. Chechnya.[17] These myths and stories are often emphatic references to events that took place in the distant past, the introduction of national anthems, a revamping of folk music, the 'rediscovery' of national flags and emblems and attempts to upgrade local dialect to a 'language'.

These means are employed in conscious attempts by political leaders (e.g. the Serbian leader Milosevic) to whip up their followers against others. They make use of modern means of communication, such as radio stations, papers and nowadays, also the Internet. During the Kosovo conflict in 1999, there were frequent references in the Serbian press to the Battle of the Blackbird Field, an event that took place in the 14th century (13 June 1389!). In this battle, the Serbs were defeated by the advancing Ottomans. This defeat — according to some Internet sites in 2004 — still had to be revenged on the Albanians, for they are the heirs of the Ottoman Empire. The Serbian 'marriage of the century', too, on Sunday, 19 February 1995 of the (late) leader of an infamous paramilitary unit and a Serbian 'turbo-folk' singer should be viewed in this context. In particular, the traditional Serbian military attire of the groom, with all the traditional decorations left little room for misinterpretation. Nor did the way in which the wedding was peddled worldwide as a 'media event'. On the basis of the past, symbols are created and traditions invented that are aimed to give insecure and fearful people a beacon for the near and far future.[18]

Category and group formation as well as stereotyping are usually processes with manipulative, but always dynamic aspects. The political leader gives his group a name and the other group a counter name on the basis of hitherto irrelevant facts. But this process of stereotyping is inevitably reciprocal. Consequently, a process of polarisation of group formation emerges, in which the unique qualities of one's own group are increasingly stressed and the demands to other groups are steadily increased. This is called 'ethnic outbidding'; it forms the basis for the escalation in the construction of political ideologies. No political leader wants to be outdone by the other in this respect.

It resembles a sort of auction in which both parties start carefully and present information on intentions and ambitions ever so warily, or even not at all. But gradually, the battle heats up and the bidding begins. This does not necessarily have to happen consciously in all cases. It may even happen unawares, such as during a reception where people begin to talk louder and louder for the simple reason that other groups of people (have to) converse in a louder voice too. This 'reception effect' is much more innocent in its intent than the 'auction' mentioned above, but the final result is the same.[19] Eventually, both parties end up in a situation of undisguised hostility. Once they have arrived at this point, it is not easy to assume a moderate position again. This self-propelling process of ideological escalation has been observed repeatedly in the many conflicts of the 1990s.[20]

Hot November in the Netherlands

Although the November weather was cold and rainy, it turned out to be a hot month in the Netherlands. On 2 November 2004, the well-known film director Theo van Gogh was killed in full daylight in the streets of Amsterdam. The perpetrator used a pistol and finished the job with knife stabs. He left two notes behind, one saying that he was prepared to die as a martyr, the other threatening the life of other public figures that had criticised Islam. Van Gogh had been among those Islam-bashing persons, who had persistently used the media to call Muslims by the most appalling of insults, 'goat fuckers'. The killer, who was arrested immediately afterwards, was of Moroccan descent but born in the Netherlands. He turned out to be connected to Moroccan and Syrian terrorists involved in the Casablanca and Madrid bombings some time earlier.

In the bewilderment and uproar immediately after the killing, Vice Prime Minister Zalm stated that 'from now on we are at war...'. This statement became a self-fulfilling prophecy. In the following nights, more than ten attacks on Mosques and Islamic schools took place, the most serious one completely burning down an Islamic school. At the same time, a handful of explosions in Christian churches occurred. Fortunately, no one was hurt or killed in any of the attacks. In a bungled arrest of two fellow terrorists in The Hague, the suspects threw two hand grenades. On the web, a pro-Al Qa'ida group threatened the Netherlands with more attacks, if the hostilities against Islam did not stop immediately. At least some 'original' Dutch people claimed that the attacks on the Mosques and Islamic schools were committed by Muslims themselves...

These events show that even a peaceful country may be confronted with high impact assassination, ethnic outbidding and increasing levels of nationwide violence of two polarising parties. Even in a civilised society like the Netherlands, the control of violence may drop back abruptly, if the conditions exist. On the other hand, amidst all the violence, the only fatality was Theo van Gogh. This shows that the police had no wish to kill the 'enemy', that the martyrs were not really prepared to sacrifice themselves and that the unhinged youngsters of the White Power movement, who claimed most of the attacks, only targeted buildings and not people. Hence, a certain level of civilisation was retained even during these appalling scenes. The events also show that internal strife often has international connections. For the Netherlands, there was an important message — expression of speech and tolerance, precious assets of democracy — should not be mixed up with humiliation and belittling of population groups.

At the end of the month, the tensions decreased, but psychologists claimed that the mental damage inflicted on the people involved may last for years... However, in a fundraising campaign for the Tsunami flooding in January 2005, a Moroccan-Dutch rap singer performed together with two 'original' Dutch popular music artists. The show was broadcast nationwide and it created an enormous degree of enthusiasm among the population at large.

What is striking here is that the differences that give so much cause for conflict are basically relatively minor. The smaller the differences between the groups, the greater the conflicts, it seems. Of course, as the conflict develops, the differences are (made) bigger. In the Sudan, there was (and is) not only tension between the Islamic North and the Christian South, but there were also regular conflicts of old between the various Southern tribes. Among Muslims, the differences between Sunnis and Shiites lead to persistent conflicts. In countries like Pakistan, these conflicts induce appalling violence of one group against another, as happened for instance, in October 2004, when 39 people died and hundreds were wounded as the result of a car bombing.[21] This strife between more or less similar groups is the same as the violent conflicts between Catholics and Protestants in Northern Ireland that have occurred over the past few decades. 'Narcissism of minor differences' can lead to great conflicts, precisely because people sense that small differences are an implied criticism of themselves and hence want to safeguard their own identity.[22]

But this process occurs even without the political ideologies of the leaders. In de Swaan's words, '... most of all, every group name evokes its opposite'. Where an armed gang calls itself Croat of whatever sort, the people in the area know they have to fear for their possessions and even for dear life if they are Serbs, and it makes them conscious of being Serbs.[23] Gradually, violence begets counter violence, for stereotyping forbids pity for others outside the group. The effect of the Thomas rule in 'ordinary people conflicts' is yet again illustrated with this.

Violence begets counter violence and then again new violence, so that nothing remains but one great entanglement of fighting parties, especially once the leaders have provided their followers with weapons. In these situations, the positions of perpetrators and victims are permanently exchanged. This was (and is) the case in Bosnia, Rwanda, Liberia, the Congo, the Sudan, Sri Lanka, the Moluccans and so many other places around the globe. The only way to distinguish the fighting parties is by the opinions and ideas they ventilate about themselves and about the 'enemy'. Stereotypes and related political ideologies, in other words, are more than just words and hollow phrases. They are consciously intended as discriminatory and harbour the danger of actually creating the reality they are 'describing'.

Notes

1. The main reasoning in this chapter is based on Soeters J. and van Twuyver, M., National and ethnic stereotyping in organizations, in Barfoot C.C. (ed.), *Beyond Pug's Tour. National and Ethnic Stereotyping in Theory and Literary Practice*, RDC Books, Amsterdam and Atlanta, 495–510, 1997; Hewstone M. and Brown R. (eds.), *Contact and Conflict in Intergroup Encounters*, Basil Blackwell,

Oxford, 1986; Hogg M.A. and Abrams, D., *Social Identifications. A Social Psychology of Intergroup Relations and Group Processes*, Routledge, London, 1988.

2. For example, Horowitz, D.L., op. cit., 46, 1985.

3. de Temmerman, E., op. cit., 82 and 247ff, 1994. See also de Swaan, A., *Uitdijende kringen van desidentificatie: gedachten over Rwanda* (Widening circles of dysidentification: reflections on Rwanda), *Amsterdams Sociologisch Tijdschrift*, 24, 3–23, 1997 A bewildering novel about how obscurity about someone's ethnical background may have fatal consequences is Courtemanche, G., *Een zondag aan het zwembad in Kigali (A Sunday at the Swimming Pool in Kigali)*, De Bezige Bij, Amsterdam, 2003; Also Gourevitch, Ph., op. cit., 47–62, 1998.

4. Ahmed, A., *Discovering Islam. Making Sense of Muslim History and Society*, Routledge, London, 123, 2003. For more examples of colonial practices leading to ethnic nepotism, see Horowitz, D.L., op. cit., 159–160, 1985.

5. This text is based on Wheatcroft, A., op. cit., 102–103 and 200–202, 2004; Buruma I. and Margalit, A., *Occidentalism. The West in the Eyes of its Enemies*, Penguin, New York, 10–11, 2004; Lewis, B., *What Went Wrong? Western Impact and Middle Eastern Response*, Phoenix, London, 2002.

6. Merton, R.K., *Social Theory and Social Structure*, McMillan, New York, 480ff, 1968.

7. Merton, R.K., op. cit., 475ff, 1968; de Swaan, A., op. cit., 37–39, 1996. About the example of the 'Tutsification' of Rwanda, see de Temmernan, E., op. cit., 247–249, 1994; de Swaan, A., op. cit., 1997.

8. Hodson, R., Sekulic D. and Massey, G., op. cit., 1550, 1994.

9. Pyszynski, T., Solomon S. and Greenberg, J., *In the Wake of 9/11. The Psychology of Terror*, American Psychological Association, Washington DC, 2003.

10. de Swaan, A., op. cit., 15, 1997; for the characterisation of Tutsis as devils, see Gourevitch, Ph., op. cit., 94, 1998. About the Russian way of stereotyping people from Chechnya, see Bennett, V., op. cit., 4–6, 2001.

11. Hogg, M.A., and Abrams, D., op. cit., 1988; Horowitz, D.L., op. cit., 29, 1985.

12. See for instance, the predictive articles of Yugoslav sociologist Tomasic in Tomasic, D., Sociology in Yougoslavia, *American Journal of Sociology*, 47, 53–69, 1941; The structure of Balkan society, *American Journal of Sociology*, 52, 132–140, 1946. See also Ugresic, D., op. cit., 1995. On the violent role of religions, see Collins, R., op. cit., especially pages 423–430, 1974.

13. This concept is developed by Castells, M., *The Power of Identity* (sec. edn), Blackwell, Oxford, 2004.

14. This section is based on de Swaan, A., op. cit., 4–5, 1997. In connection with this, see also Castells, M., op. cit., 2004.

15. Barth F. (ed.), *Ethnic Groups and Boundaries*, University Press, Oslo, 1969; Also Williams, B.F., A class act: anthropology and the race to nation across ethnic terrain, *Annual Review of Anthropology*, 18, 401–441, 1989; Eisenstadt S.N. and Giesen, B., The construction of collective identity, *European Journal of Sociology*, 36, 72–102, 1995; McAdam D., et al., op. cit., 142, 2001.

16. Marwell, G., Oliver P.E. and Prahl, R., Social networks and collective action: a theory of the critical mass. III, *American Journal of Sociology*, 94, 502–534,

1988. See also McAdam D., *et al.*, op. cit., 58–60, 2001. It has been noticed that throughout history, political parties and terrorist groups have been going hand in hand, like, currently, the IRA and Sinn Fein in Northern Ireland. See Weinberg L. and Pedahzur, A., *Political Parties and Terrorist Groups*, Routledge, London and New York, 2003.

17.   Tishkov, V., op. cit., 51, 2004.

18.   See Hobsbawm E. and Ranger, T., *The Invention of Tradition*, Cambridge University Press, Cambridge, 1984. This, however, only refers to cultural elements that are relatively superficial. The cultural core, i.e. the values, that has been discussed in Chapter 5 is less susceptible to manipulation by political leaders. See also Gagnon V.P. Jr., op. cit., 1994 about the manipulative role of the political elite in the Bosnian conflict. See also Gellner, E., *Nations and Nationalism*, Blackwell, Oxford, 48–49, 1983.

19.   Goudsblom, J., *Het regime van de tijd (The Regime of Time)*, Meulenhoff, Amsterdam, 88–89, 1997.

20.   Kaufman, S.J., op. cit., 111, 1996; see also Lake D.A. and Rothchild, D., op. cit., 54, 1996.

21.   Anonymous (Reuters), *Pakistan verbiedt openbare bijeenkomsten na bomaanslag* (Pakistan forbids public gatherings after bomb attack), *Volkskrant*, 8 October 2004.

22.   Blok, A., op. cit., 115–135, 2001; Horowitz, D.L., op. cit., 182, 1985. The concept of 'narcissism of minor differences' was coined by Sigmund Freud.

23.   de Swaan, A., De staat van wandaad. Over de verrvagende grezen tussen oorlogvoering en misdaadbestrijding (The state of Misdeed. About the warring and crimefighting), *Twee stukken (Two Pieces)*, Het spintiuis, Amsterdam, 1–14, 1994. Also, see Collins, R., op. cit., 417, 1974.

8

SOCIAL MOBILISATION AND LEADERSHIP

The process of group formation, stereotyping and ideologising described above can be relatively unstructured, amorphous and not always clearly discernible. But it often deepens and then becomes more serious. What emerges is a social movement as it were, that really opens the floodgates for violence and conflict.

Outbreaks of violence resulting from the internal conflicts discussed in this book are expressions of collective action. They relate to the actions of a collective of people, rallied round a group identity and a mission,[1] usually originating from a feeling of uneasiness — the loss of power, economic decline or discontent due to the loss of ideals such as national independence. In order to curb this feeling of uneasiness, the mission, a political ambition, is formulated. This is comparable to what was called political ideology in the previous chapter. Such a mission or political ideology can be directed at the creation of an independent nation, the reparation of former power relations, the restoration of administrative autonomy, the attainment of 'heaven on earth' or the realisation of 'ethnic purity'. The mission is an expression of an extreme idolisation of the aim that can manifest itself in collective utopias, social myths and the 'mobilisation of fantasy'.[2] The supporters pledge allegiance to the ideal formulated by the political elite — the nation, one's own people, the war, one's own religion, the reconstruction, etc.

Such social movements are characterised by an increase of human energy. People are involved in the movement, feverishly and all-out. There is a kind of collective ecstasy. Every bit of energy they can bring to bear — and that is often considerably more than the usual 100% — is devoted exclusively to the great ideal. Social movements have such important tasks to fulfil that they cannot be bothered with *Alltagswirtschaft* (everyday economic matters). The fact that the economy suffers in times of violence and conflict has, most certainly, not only to do with the shelling and bombing of factories and offices. There is also this other point that everyday duties, such as school and work, are neglected, for they are not deemed important anymore. Technical and bureaucratic skills of people are brushed aside as

~ Think in terms of cun of cas

irrelevant. In the light of the great ideal, everyone is equal. It is for this reason that people in the movement wear uniform dress, if not real uniforms. Besides, these movements are characterised by a certain *Familienfremdheit* (alienation of the family). Relations with family and relatives are of secondary importance to working for the great ideal. Men and boys join the battle in times of conflict and the women at the home front are left to fend for themselves.

A final feature is that social movements almost always follow a certain pattern. The most important fact here is that social movements as such are finite. As fast and violent as their ascent is, as certain is their fading after some time. They either abolish themselves after some time, which will happen when success remains elusive, or they institutionalise and routinise when the aim or an otherwise stable situation has been attained. What follows is consolidation; the 'magic of the movement' has faded and an everyday routine sets in. After all, one has to make a living. Insofar as social mobilisation is connected with violence, the finiteness of social movements is an important and positive factor. At some point in time, the violence will end (until it flares up again).[3]

Social movement and violence

It is important to realise that these characteristics are applicable to all social (idealistic, political or religious) movements and therefore, also to political parties, Greenpeace, Amnesty International, *Médecins sans Frontières*, the Baghwan movement, the Animal Liberation Front, the *Rote Armee Fraktion*, the *Sendero Luminoso* from Peru, the liberation movements for a free Basque province, a free Corsica, an ethnically pure Serbia, an independent Palestine, the *Jihad* movement, etc. These examples clearly show that not all social movements are violent. But, in any case, these movements are quite demanding of their members.

This fact has prompted sociologist Collins to remark that social (political, religious) movements 'commit violence internally, directed at their members'. Social movements demand a lot of their members, such as extreme loyalty, a 'pure conscience', high subscription fees (often a considerable part of their salary), denial of pleasures (no sex, no individual clothing, no make-up, etc.). In fact, what is required of the members is a form of asceticism, but in the more extreme cases of religious sects, the movement demands considerably more; for instance, sexual submission to the leader and sometimes even sacrificing one's life.[4]

The fatal vicissitudes of religious sects in Waco (Texas), Switzerland, Canada and California illustrate the extent to which a social movement can be tied up with internally directed violence. These examples, in which scores of people died, all date back to the 1990s, the last one as late as 1997. In the 1970s, there was a different, particularly spectacular example of violence within a religious movement. It concerns the collective suicide of 913 followers of American preacher Jim Jones, who lived in a commune (a 'concentration camp' in the eyes of some), somewhere in South America. The pattern in this kind of event is that the sect is threatened by the outside world at some point in time — usually the government that has been mobilised by worried relatives. This violation of community life is answered by the destruction of the entire community and all its members; men, women and children. On the authority of the leader, the followers commit suicide — the poisoned cup a clear favourite — and those who refuse are helped on their way. Loyal following of orders is transformed into coercion. Suicide becomes homicide.[5]

It is striking that this phenomenon seems to occur especially in countries with very strong individualistic cultures, such as the USA, Canada and Switzerland. Apparently, the sects in these countries function as a collectivist 'reservoir' — mother's lap, if you please — for persons who cannot cope with an individualistic society and hence, become unhinged and marginalised. The movements themselves are naturally very collectivist, but they conform to the individualistic character of the society that spawns them; in that they do not interact with that wider society. As a result, the movements or sects remain focussed on themselves. So, they are movements or sects that exert internally directed violence on a relatively small scale. This is the first form of exertion of violence by social movements.

In the second combination of violence and collective mobilisation, the exertion of violence is also relatively small-scale, but directed externally. The line between internally and externally directed violence is crossed and outsiders are targeted. One example is the criminal gangs in American cities that give shelter to unhinged and neglected youths by offering them an alternative way of life and not infrequently, by creating a collective enemy (whites, cops, the gang in the other neighbourhood, etc.).

Another example is the behaviour of the paramilitias in the USA that turn against the government and do not hesitate to commit bombing attacks, causing many casualties, such as the case in the Oklahoma bombing in 1995. The 'small scale' of this kind of violence does not so much refer to the extent of the damage that is inflicted, but to its incidental character. This has to do with the relatively limited number of 'recruits' that these movements manage to attract. Needless to say, they are usually marginalised members of society. Obviously, these movements mainly operate in concealment and clandestinely.

There are indications that the number of violent groups of an extreme right wing, anti-government nature is steadily rising, both in Western countries and in Russia. Often, these movements also find inspiration in a sort of Christian fundamentalism that, for instance, rejects abortion; clinics in America are regularly targeted in violent attacks. In relation to this, mention is made of the possible return of the 'conservative revolution', a reversal of the political — left wing — violence occurring in countries such as Germany and Italy in the 1970 and 1980s. This type of leftist movement, incidentally, is still active in South America, as was illustrated by the mass hostage-taking in Lima during the turn of the year 1996–1997.[6]

Yet another variant of outwardly directed, relatively small-scale violence is the so-called sectarian violence. It comes from small movements that have turned away from society, have no political mission, but do have a (religious) messianic mission. Around the turn of the millennium, there was an increase in the number of sects that preached the end of the world. In the sociology of religion, such phenomena are described as 'millennarianism'; they occur at the turn of almost every century or millennium. Based on a sort of 'demon thinking', these sects do not hesitate to use violence against the 'perverted' society, which after all, does not want to hear of any repentance or reflection on the approaching end. In March 1995, one such sect committed a nerve gas attack on the passengers of the Tokyo metro, killing several and wounding many.[7]

The third combination of violence and collective mobilisation is also directed externally, but it is clearly large-scale. More people are involved, including people other than the pure insiders from the movement. The social movement leaves its isolation behind and becomes a mass movement. Modern means of communication (radio, television, the Internet) are employed to win large numbers of people over for an ideal that, from societal, religious and cultural backgrounds, acquires a more explicit, intentional political meaning. This is nothing new. In the Indonesian freedom movement (1945–1949), the Islamic factions belonged to the most fanatical fighters for the political goal of independence.[8]

In the present day violence, the combination of religious and political backgrounds plays an important role. To prove this point, it only takes a reference to Afghanistan during the Taliban regime (until 2002 and after), as well as Pakistan and Chechnya, where Islamic movements want to make short shrift of everything with even a whiff of the Western and the modern (the godless, women, homosexuals). In the Sudan, a rebel religious sect of Christian signature, 'The Resistance Army of the Lord' was (and is) armed in order to spread death and destruction among the rural population in the Islamic North of the country.[9]

Initially, this increase in scale causes terrorism and guerrilla warfare, but eventually they spawn the real conflicts and wars of the extent discussed in this book.[10] When, why and how this increase in scale takes place (eventually leading to violent conflicts as in Somalia, Rwanda and Bosnia) depends on a number of factors. Among them is the mission or ideology of the movement and several others that have been mentioned above, such as national culture, the functioning of the monopoly of violence, aggressive stereotyping, etc.

The wrath of God... [11]

Violent religious movements are on the rise. They find their origin in all religions — Christianity (attacks on abortion clinics), Judaism (Baruch Goldstein's attack on praying Muslims in Jerusalem), Hinduism (many acts of violence in India) and Islam (the Jihad, 9/11, Istanbul). The conflict in the Balkans was and is being fought on religious terms between Catholic Croats, Orthodox Serbs and Islamic Bosnians. Now that the war is over, the first priorities in rebuilding the country lie with churches and mosques, often very close to each other..., and virtually in all cases, funded by money from outside the country. In Northern Ireland, Catholics and Protestants fought each other as if they were still living in the days of the iconoclastic fury...

This religious revival must be related to a general sense of discontent with existing power relations (the Palestinians up against Israel), past and present humiliation ('Mad Mullah', 'goat fuckers') and economic inequality. It is also a reaction against globalisation. In a time of overpopulation, poverty, social uprooting in the big cities, the nasty challenges of Western materialism that is visible but intangible (beautiful half-naked women on billboards), people look for targets, direction and meaning in their lives. Religion offers all this, even if it implies the rejection of the dominant West ('we will be modern, but we won't be you'), if necessary, even with violence.

Religious violence is committed by pious, decent people, who are certainly not 'mad', but fully convinced of their moral righteousness. They are the people who stand for 'old, fundamental values and religious convictions'. This certainty leads them to wage a 'cosmic' war, that is, a war that goes beyond the here and now. In it, personal dignity is leading; loss and defeat are unthinkable and the firm conviction that there is no other way of fighting this battle anymore has taken hold. These people then become martyrs, who think they know for sure that they will spend the rest of their lives in the eternal bliss of the hereafter. Usually they are young men of some military skill. They are increasingly being joined by young women who have lost members of their families. More often than not, they are youth from destitute backgrounds, with a first-hand experience of poverty (in some cases the next of kin are given an allowance).

In each of the above-mentioned types of violence and collective mobilisation, the members of the movement are incited by the dynamics of the social mobilisation, or put under great pressure to commit acts of violence. Hardly anybody will do this completely out of free will. Without the 'fever' and the pressure of the movement, the violence in Rwanda, Bosnia or Chechnya is unthinkable.

This is even truer for the last and fourth form of collective mobilisation and violence — the one in which internally and externally directed violence coincides. The result is suicide commandos, the best-known example of which is the Japanese Kamikaze pilots of World War II. Descriptions of their mindset clearly show that there was heavy pressure on the sense of honour of these young men, which subsequently threw them in a violent internal conflict. Those who did not 'need' to join up anymore because of the end of the war, were extremely relieved.[12]

Other examples of the fatal combination of internally and externally directed violence are the continuous assaults in Israel's streets and of course, the attacks on the Twin Towers as well as the various attacks in Russia (by Chechen rebels). In the Indonesian struggle for independence, there were many attacks on the Dutch positions that cannot be called anything other than collective suicides. They often cost hundreds, if not thousands, of casualties among the freedom fighters, with only a few on the Dutch side.[13]

These suicide actions are executed in the firm conviction that they guarantee a place in heaven. In sociology, this is called the '*suicide altruiste*', the suicide for the 'others', the 'collective', or the 'movement'. After all, the ultimate collective movement wastes the lives of others as well as its own.[14]

Violence and leadership

It is important to realise that collective mobilisation almost always develops under the impulses of a leading group, led by a charismatic or prophetic leader.[15] Charisma can be defined as the talent to emotionally enthral, fix and captivate followers, the talent to tempt people or to mesmerise them, if you please. The prophet or charismatic leader has a messianic message, a god-given commandment. He or she manages to generate a form of mass hysteria or collective ecstasy, making the followers believe in the most unbelievable things, even in their invulnerability, which was the case, for instance, in the Indonesian struggle for independence.[16] There is no cure against a charismatic leader. Critical notes, however realistic and sober minded, are ignored, jeered at and laughed away or even suppressed with violence. It is not surprising that extreme forms of charismatic leadership particularly occur in cultures with large power distances, a large degree of uncertainty avoidance and strong collectivism, to speak in terms of Chapter 5.

In this type of culture, great leaders can cherish a prophet's aureole and boast divinity, or at least close contact with God. History is replete with examples, from the Roman emperors (Caligula, Nero) to Hitler, Stalin, Mao Ze Dong and Osama Bin Laden. These great leaders were, and are, worshipped and cheered as persons with enormous appeal, including sexual — Hitler was *Führer*, but also *Verführer*, the great tempter. But sometimes, they are literally seen as representatives of God. There are enough testimonies that show that people prayed, in the most literal sense of the word, to portraits and photographs of Hitler.

In the conflict in the former Yugoslavia, the political leaders played a similar 'holy' role. Izetbegovic, Milosevic and Tudzjman were treated as prophets with messianic teachings. They were seen as saviours of their country and people. Anyone who ventured to voice criticism would be publicly reprimanded. This was reported by observers of various sides, including the Dutch General Brinkman.[17] Osama Bin Laden only speaks in the name of Allah, as if he is in personal contact with him. The leaders in the Southern parts of the Sudan also play an extremely dominant role in mobilising their ranks and files.[18]

The question whether the charismatic leader is absolutely necessary, or replaceable for the social movement, cannot be answered in general. Of course it is hindsight, but it is certainly not unthinkable that Germany without Hitler would have gone adrift in the 1930s and 1940s, anyway. After all, this is what the country had done in World War I. But without Hitler, a number of aspects of World War II, such as the fixation on the Jewish citizens, might have gone differently. Sebastian Haffner, in a mental experiment, once voiced the supposition that Hitler, had he been killed in the 1938 assassination attempt, would have been considered one of Germany's greatest statesmen in the eyes of many.[19]

In other words, it is too psychological and simple to attribute the behaviour of the Germans during World War II wholly to Hitler (or in corresponding cases, Stalin or Saddam Hussein). On the other hand, it is too sociological and simple to say, given the social dynamics and circumstances of that time, that Hitler could have been replaced by any other leader. In understanding the role of leaders in conflicts, it is always a matter of an interaction between sociological conditions and psychological personality traits. Both factors (and of course, chance), with mutual dynamics of their own, create the eventual actual events.

With regard to the personality traits of leaders in conflicts (and, incidentally, also of leaders in general), there is one other aspect worth mentioning.[20] Great leaders have flair; they are extrovert, communicative and flirtatious. It is these qualities, generally experienced as signs of self-awareness and self-confidence that brought them to the top. But once there, the danger exists that they spread insidiously without check and degenerate into a pathological phenomenon — narcissism, or being in love with oneself. Narcissistic leaders behave in an exhibitionist manner. They love pomp and circumstance — parties, shows, parades and demonstrations. They surround themselves with uncritical followers, sycophants and flatterers who often even identify in their outward appearance (uniform, hair style, moustache, etc.) with the great leader. It is striking to see how Saddam was always accompanied by men (civilians and military) who, in their outward appearance, were almost clones of the great leader himself. The need for flattery reinforces itself and becomes addictive. In this way, a pathology, or psychological disease, can develop in the interplay between leader and followers.[21] The leader or hero thinks the world of him or herself, an idea that is reinforced by the followers who idolise and worship him or her. This *folie à deux* works as a self-winding spring. But in the end, the spring reaches the point of breaking. Narcissistic leaders then steadily lose sympathy for their followers and abuse their loyalty. Abuse of power is rampant. The leaders openly and shamelessly bestow favours on members of their own family and clan. People outside the inner circle do not count. Subordinates are played off against each other and pushed into mutual competition, in the extreme cases, until death follows. It is not difficult to recognise in this description the behaviour of leaders in many historical and present day conflict situations.

Notes

1. The following is based on elements of the work of one of the founding fathers of sociology, Max Weber. See Schreuder, O., *Sociale bewegingen, een systematische inleiding (Social Movements. A Systemactic Introduction)*, van Loghum Slaterus, Deventer, 85–87, 1981; van Doorn, J.A.A, *Met man en macht. Sociologische studies over maatschappelijke mobilisatie (With Might and Main. Sociological Studies on Societal Mobilisation)*, Boom, Meppel, 1973. See also Castells, M., op. cit., 2004.
2. de Swaan, A., op. cit., 15, 1997.
3. See also Marx G.T. and Wood, J.L., Strands of theory and research in collective behavior, *Annual Review of Sociology*, 1, 367–428, especially page 394ff, 1975. An empirical description of the temporary character of a social movement (the so-called Swing Rebellion in the UK in the 19th century) can be found in Tilly, Ch., op. cit., 178–187, 2003.
4. Collins, R., op. cit., 434–436, 1974.
5. Hall, J.R. et al., *Apocalypse Observed. Religious Movements and Violence in North America, Europe, and Japan*, Routledge, London, 2000. About organisations and institutions that 'consume' their own members, see Coser, L.A., *Greedy Institutions, Patterns of Undivided Commitment*, Free Press, New York, 1974.
6. Overdiek, T., *Milities hebben het in VS gemunt op 'regeringstirannie'* (Militias in the USA are targeting 'governmental tyranny'), *Volkskrant*, 24 April 1995, p.5; Garschagen, O., *Zwarte kerken VS zijn weer doelwit van racisten* (Black churches in the USA are once again targeted by racists), *Volkskrant*, 24 May 1996, p.6. An analysis of the possible return of extreme right movements can be found in Dahl, G., Will 'the other God' fail again? On the possible return of the

conservative revolution, *Theory, Culture and Society*, 13, 25–50, 1996. See also Juergensmeyer, M., op. cit., 2000.

7. Hall, J.R. *et al.*, op. cit., 2000; Juergensmeyer, M., op. cit., 2000. See also Kaplan, J. (ed.), *Millennial Violence. Past, Present and Future*, Frank Cass, London, 2002.

8. van Doorn, J.A.A. and Hendrix, W.J., op. cit., 138, 1970.

9. Lanting, B., *In heroverd Grozny heerst de Islamitische wet* (In reconquered Grozny Islamic law rules), *Volkskrant*, 24 September 1996, p.4; Anonymous, *Zwartgemaakte homo's rondgereden door Kabul* (Maligned gays driven around in Kabul), *Volkskrant*, 27 December 1996; Anonymous, *Taliban jagen burgers van Kabul de moskee in* (Taliban drives citizens of Kabul into the Mosque), *Volkskrant*, 5 October 1996, p.1; Heyzer, N., *Belofte aan Afghaanse vrouwen moet worden nagekomen* (Promise to Afghan women should be kept), *Volkskrant*, 4 December 2003; Bond, C., *Bewind Sudan bewapent rebelse sekte in noorden van Sudan* (Sudan regime arms rebellious sect in Northern Sudan), *Volkskrant*, 2 April 1996. About Chechnya, see Winslow, D. and Moelker, R., op. cit., 2002; Tishkov, V., op. cit., 164–179, 2004.

10. Teitler, G., op. cit., 1972.

11. This section is based on Juergensmeyer, M., op. cit., 2000; Huntington, S., op. cit., 1996; Castells, M., op. cit., 2004; Tibi, B., op. cit., 2002; Sells, M., *The Bridge Betrayed. Religion and Genocide in Bosnia*, University of California Press, Berkeley, 1998; Armstrong, K., *The Battle for God*, Knopf, New York, 2000; Pamuk, O., The anger of the damned, *New York Review of Books*, 15 November 2001; Stern, J., op. cit., 2003.

12. Nagatsuka, R., *I was a Kamikaze pilot. The knights of the divine wind*, New English Library, London, 1973. See also Ohnuki-Tierney, E., *Kamikaze, Cherry Blossoms, and Nationalisms*, The University of Chicago Press, Chicago, 2002. See also Buruma, I. and Margalit, A., op. cit., Chapter 3, 2002.

13. van Doorn, J.A.A. and Hendrix, W.J., op. cit., 140, 1970.

14. The concept of '*suicide altruiste*' originates from one of the founding fathers of sociology, Emile Durkheim.

15. Weber, M., *The Sociology of Religion*, Methuen & Co, London, in particular Chapter 4, 1963.

16. van Doorn, J.A.A. and Hendrix, W.J., op. cit., 138, 1970.

17. Anonymous, *Kans op nieuwe strijd Bosnië fifty-fifty* (Probability of new struggle in Bosnia fifty-fifty), *Volkskrant*, 4 March 1995. See also Ugresic, D., op. cit., 1995.

18. Madut Jok, J. and Hutchinson, S.E., Sudan's prolonged second civil war and the militarisation of Nuer and Dinka identities, *African Studies Review*, 42, 125–145, 1999.

19. Haffner, S., *Anmerkungen zu Hitler (Observations on Hitler)*, Kindler, München, 1978.

20. The following is based on Kets de Vries, M. and Miller, D., *The Neurotic Organization: Diagnosing and Changing Counterproductive Styles of Management*, Jossey-Bass, San Francisco, 1984. See also Kets de Vries, M., *Leaders*,

Fools and Impostors. Essays on the Psychology of Leadership, Jossey-Bass, San Francisco, 1993; Kets de Vries, M., *Organisational Paradoxes. Clinical Approaches to Management*, Routledge, London, in particular Chapter 7, 1995.
21. The former Chechen leader Dudajev has often been described as being psychologically unstable and even completely mad. See Tishkov, V., op. cit., 77, 2004.

9

RISING EXPECTATIONS, RELATIVE DEPRIVATION AND REDUCTION OF POWER DISTANCE

In the study of social movements and conflicts, there is a curious phenomenon. Not those who are the most deprived from an objective point of view, but especially those who have already tasted a larger piece of the cake, feel the most that they have been treated unfairly. This fact is perhaps not entirely contrary to what many, Marxist theoreticians among them, think, but it is at least a complication in their ideas.

These ideas draw attention to the conflict of class and interests, in which one category of people (for instance, the 'merchants' or the 'large landowners') exploit other categories, in particular, the unpropertied. In this line of reasoning, the underlying group or groups will resort to violence when this exploitation has crossed a certain limit and 'enough is enough'. According to these theories, once the subordinate group becomes aware of the extent of exploitation, the time is ripe for action. This point is comparable to the boiling point in physics — up to one hundred degrees centigrade the heating process changes only gradually, but at the boiling point there is a rapid change. Empirical research, however, shows that the social dynamics follow a different, or at least more complex, pattern. Studies of ethnic conflicts show that, of the supposed causes of violence and conflict, not a single one explicitly 'referred to economic grievances against any of the named ethnic groups'. Reproaches against the higher classes are almost always couched in political terms and especially make an appearance during election campaigns. The ensuing violence is hardly ever (solely) committed by the poorest of the poor.[1] This is, in fact, a global phenomenon.

What is striking is that the poor, ordinary people in traditional societies are usually resigned to their fate and have not the slightest inclination to take action. To some extent, this is caused by admiration for those in power ('the nobility is a different, superior species'), and a sort of resignation ('nothing can be done about it, anyway'; 'it's all the same'). But there is also some well-understood self-interest ('the landowner is our protector') and contempt for the upper classes ('we would not want to have their worries in any case').[2] Sheer poverty, such as the pariahs in India, usually does not lead to action and violence. What, then, is the relation between economic relations and the balances of power, on the one hand, and the outbreaks of violent conflicts, on the other?

The answer to this question begins with the realisation that most conflicts break out at the very moment that people are doing relatively well. These improvements in their situation have come about after periods of stable but low-level prosperity or political freedom. As a result of social and economic prosperity, people have begun to cherish higher expectations of the future. They may even have begun to compare themselves with groups that seemed unreachable hitherto. It is also possible that a reference group, a group that has always been considered comparable to them, has gone through such a social, political or economic ascent. Thus, the point of reference, the group with which one compares oneself, or the ambitions that may reasonably be cherished, shifts. These situations have been shown to have the potential to lead to violent conflicts. This sometimes seemingly paradoxical phenomenon has already been described more than a hundred and fifty years ago by French sociologist Alexis de Tocqueville in his analysis of the French Revolution.

More precisely, this phenomenon encompasses four patterns, which can be gathered under the common denominator of 'collective frustration'.[3]

A. A group sees opportunities for moving on because a new ideology promises new chances, or it comes into contact with a new way of life (for instance, with more chances of promotion, more income, the Western life style, or political autonomy). If, in the course of time, a gap develops between expectations and reality, then frustration emerges; this is called the dynamics of 'rising expectations'.

B. A group begins to compare itself with another group in society that is economically, culturally and politically more successful; as a result of this comparison, the group feels deprived; this phenomenon is called the pattern of 'relative deprivation'.

C. A group experiences 'status inconsistency', because it contributes a lot to society economically, but in a political-administrative sense it has no, or little, say in matters.

D. A group has flourished for some time, but during a certain period there is a (temporary) 'decline' in prosperity.

In Figure 8, these four patterns are presented graphically. It is important to note that in all patterns (also C and D) 'rising expectations' and 'relative deprivation' are key elements. So, relative deprivation, in general, refers to feelings of deprivation in comparison to something else (another group, a different sector of society, or a comparison with the recent past). In all cases, there is a gap between ambition and reality, which in a number of cases leads to frustration and motivates action and violence.

100

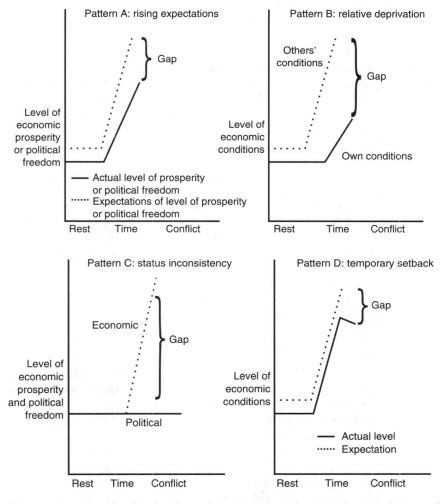

Figure 8 Patterns of collective frustration. Source: Coleman, J.S., *Foundations of Social Theory*, Belknap Press, Cambridge, MA, 1994; copyright Harvard University Press.

There are many examples of pattern A. The Indonesian independence movement originated when the Dutch colonisers had been driven out by the Japanese occupying force and, as a result, the perspective of a greater Asian self-confidence and self-rule emerged. Already, after six months of Japanese occupation, a change in the mentality of the indigenous population began to appear. 'The self-respect, which in Dutch colonial times was not visible among our people, now grew little by little' — according to

101

an Indonesian resident, who, incidentally, was not known as a friend of the Japanese.[4] The popularity of the Hitler regime prior to the outbreak of World War II was partially related to the prospect of a better life (work, income, etc.) promised by the Nazis.

Rising expectations in themselves are not a reason for conflict and violence, but they will become just that when they are frustrated by external circumstances or by some other group. Then, the gap between (rising) expectations and the possibilities to realise them will steadily increase. A classic example is the hanging parties in the southern states of the USA whenever the cotton harvest fell short of expectations. The German Nazi regime did not really become dangerous for the rest of Europe until the 'dreams' of Hitler and his clique became increasingly ambitious and, by definition, could no longer be realised on Germany's own territory. The limits of their own territory, in other words, the presence of other nation states, frustrated these ambitious expectations. Conversely, the velvet and silent revolutions that took place in the Eastern European countries in 1989 were a direct consequence of rising expectations that caught on from one country onto the next through the mass media. But since these rising expectations were met, these revolutions were almost completely peaceful, with the exception of Rumania. Thus, there was no gap between expectations and the possibilities to realise them.[5] The independence movements on the flanks of the former Soviet Union were instigated by declarations of Russian democrats in the early 1990s, who preached the virtue of ethno-national self-determination. This Perestroika ideology led people to believe that independence would create a better, more prosperous life in those areas.[6] When the goal of independence was reached easily, like in the Baltic region, no violence whatsoever occurred. If however, like in Chechnya, the expectations were frustrated, then violence struck.

An illustration of pattern B can be found in the well-known study of Samuel Stouffer on the 'American Soldier'. Stouffer and his team found that morale (atmosphere, group motivation) among officers of the Military Police was better than among Air Force officers. This was peculiar, as the opportunities for promotion in the Air Force were considerably better than in the Military Police. Many officers in the Air Force were promoted quickly. The explanation for the low morale was found in the relative deprivation of the group of Air Force officers that had not come up for promotion; they saw themselves lagging behind with those of their Service that did get promoted.[7]

This situation led to discontent, but of course, not to violence. A classic example of the latter is the French Revolution. It did not begin on the instigation of the peasants, the most impoverished population category at the time, but of the so-called Third Order, the traders, craftsmen and factory owners, in short, the middle class. As it was, they felt they were falling behind with the traditionally powerful, the nobility and the clerics, in political importance. This example illustrates pattern B as well as pattern C. The Third Order compared itself with other groups (First and Second Order) and felt hard done by, all the more so since they experienced a sense of status deprivation as a result of their relatively increasing economic importance in society.[8] Other, current examples refer to the Palestinians, who compare themselves with Israeli citizens and hence feel relatively deprived with respect to job opportunities and housing facilities. Also, in the Chechen conflict, this pattern can clearly be seen — compared to the Russians, the Chechens feel dispossessed when it comes to educational facilities, employment and housing and in general, feel slighted with respect to the distribution of oil gains.[9] The same feeling of deprivation among the Southerners has instigated and fuelled the civil war in the Sudan for so many years. Not surprisingly, in the peace negotiations, an equal distribution of oil gains between North and South Sudan was one of the major controversial issues. This feeling may develop even in relief campaigns. During the campaigns to help the victims of the Tsunami flooding in January 2005, the Tamil Tigers in North Sri Lanka and the Aceh population in Indonesia accused the central governments of offering too little help, too late. They claimed this was the government's revenge against their struggle for independence.

Another clear example of pattern B (relative deprivation) is the violence that is directed — often in the context of electoral struggles — at ethnic minorities that hold the economic power in a country. The world knows many examples of such rich ethnic butts of violence, e.g. the Chinese minorities in South-East Asia (Indonesia, Malaysia, the Philippines), the rich European whites in South America, again the rich European whites in Southern Africa (Zimbabwe, South Africa, Namibia, and somewhat more to the North in Kenya), economically successful African minorities in countries such as Nigeria and Cameroon, the Indians in East Africa, the Lebanese in West Africa, and, finally, the Jewish entrepreneurs in present day Russia. The violence towards these rich minorities can adopt many guises, from 'normal' murders and downright razzias in the Chinese districts of Jakarta to the hate campaigns organised by the dominant political parties in Zimbabwe and Russia. In the latter case, the violence does not involve much blood and murder, but there is incarceration and dispossession. This, of course, is violence, too. In other cases, it may involve bloody violence, even leading to genocide.[10]

Pattern C, which is that of status inconsistency is also rich in examples — in Saudi Arabia, all political power is concentrated in the hands of a few tribes (large families). Democracy in the Western sense of the word does not exist. For many young people in this country who do not belong to these families, but who did go to university and have (prospects of) good jobs, this situation is increasingly unacceptable. They think they too contribute to the economic prosperity of the country, but find that they have no say in politics and are unable to participate in democracy. This is at least a partial explanation for the fact that nineteen out of twenty 9/11 terrorists came from this country. The subsequent bloody attacks in the country itself are of course, also related to this. At the same time, these young people hold the opinion that their country, thanks to its enormous oil supplies, is of great importance to the global economy, but that politically it has no power at all. In their eyes, their government is a puppet of the super power, America. This is also an example of pattern C, but on a somewhat different scale. A final example, this time in connection with the former Yugoslavia, concerns the relation between Serbs and Croats. Under Tito, the Serbs reaped the political fruits, while the Croats did all the work. The highway between Zagreb and Split took decades to complete, while all around Belgrade many roads were constructed, the use or necessity of which was not obvious to the Croats.[11] Eventually, this sort of resentment led to the bloody secession of Croatia.

The dynamics of the temporary regression (pattern D) is also known as reversed 'J-curve' because of its graphic form. This pattern, along with pattern A, is probably the best-known cause of conflict and violence. In the classic text on the subject it is described as follows; 'revolutions are most likely to occur when a prolonged period of objective economic and social development is followed by a short period of sharp reversal.'[12] The protest actions of the trade unions on an imminent encroachment of the so-called 'acquired rights', as occurred in January 1995 in the Dutch regional transport sector, are Dutch, but perhaps not very shocking, example of the dynamics of that 'J-curve'.

The problems in Algeria, too, are an example of the 'J-curve' pattern. After a sound economic growth as a result of large oil and gas exports, the revenues from this sector drastically decreased in the course of the years. Well over a decade ago, the one-sidedness of the economic development in Algeria became apparent relatively suddenly. Massive unemployment and raging inflation were the results. This deplorable economic situation formed, and still forms, a fertile seedbed for the internal violence in that country.

The conflicts in the former Yugoslavia can also be explained by means of the above patterns. It is very likely that a combination of patterns D and A especially applied there. The 'J-curve' was the result of the collapse of the economic system, which in the early eighties became manifest as annual inflation figures of over 1,000 percent. A widening gap between expectations and possibilities to realise them as a result of sharply rising expectations (pattern A) occurred after Tito's demise. The ensuing power vacuum fired ambitions of power among the political and social elite. As a result, the expectations of political autonomy rose considerably. Also, the rivalry between groups, related to feelings of discrimination, relative deprivation and status inconsistency (patterns B and C) played a part in all this.

Chapter 2 on the group grid model showed how the Croats felt discriminated by the Serbs, who were over-represented in countless government functions, and the above example is one of unfair distribution of government funds.[13]

A possibly even more spectacular example of the reversed 'J-curve' concerns the so-called pyramid games in Albania, immediately after communism disappeared and capitalism had free play. Certain trendy people — criminals if you please — abused the newly-won freedom to introduce this kind of games. They managed to persuade many citizens of this country, who cherished naive dreams of quick riches, to stake their entire savings. When the pyramid, as always, collapsed suddenly, credulity came to an end and collective frustration exploded. The country ran amuck, everyone stormed the former Albanian army's armouries, and got hold of a weapon with which they swarmed the streets, shooting.

In hindsight, there was also a combination of patterns that caused the violence in Rwanda. There, too, a 'J-curve' (D) was present. Since the social revolution in 1959 until the 1970s, Rwanda had done reasonably well. The country was considered a model of rural reform. Supported by considerable Western development aid, in these years, great advances were made in the improvement of the infrastructure, literacy and the increase of the GNP. This, however, could not prevent a sudden regression in the late 1980s as a result of the first energy crisis. Foreign debts, the drop in coffee and tea prices, the devaluation of the national currency (inflation!) and a decrease in employment turned economic growth into a substantial regression. These factors, in combination with the pressure of a rising population, certainly formed a breeding ground for frustration and violence.

The other patterns, in particular, rising expectations and relative deprivation, followed and subsequently set the whole thing going. The Hutus, who had for decades felt humiliated by the Tutsis and the coloniser had finally come to power in 1959. At last, a situation had come to which they, in view of their proportion in the population, had a right. But from 1990 onwards, the Tutsis who had fled the country (the Rwandan Patriotic Front) launched attacks on the government in Rwanda from neighbouring Uganda. This caused the Hutus — especially the ones from the president's north-western region — to fear that they would lose power once again. The fear of an imminent loss of possibilities to stay in power subsequently formed enough ingredients to start the upheavals.[14]

Reduction of power distance

Dutch social-psychologist Mauk Mulder has pointed out an important phenomenon that is related to the dynamics of relative deprivation. It is known as the tendency towards 'reduction of power distance'.[15]

In the chapter on national culture, the concept of power distance was already discussed. It is this same concept, the differences in power between superiors and subordinates, that is featured in this chapter.

Just like the mechanism of relative deprivation, this phenomenon was already described by French sociologist Alexis de Tocqueville in the last century, although in a primitive and rudimentary manner. In a modern version, his observation is as follows, 'We do not feel envious towards those far above us on the social scale, only towards our immediate superiors.'[16] The closer something is, the more people are inclined to make an effort to narrow the distance to it. This phenomenon is an important element in the theory of reduction of power distance. It can be compared with the task of a high jumper who wants to break a record. When the record height is only a few centimetres higher than his own achievement, he will try everything he can to bridge the small gap. When the record is several decimetres higher, he will quickly lose the courage to improve himself.

The theory on the reduction of power distance contains two key hypotheses with regard to the dynamics of power distances between people:

A. Powerful people tend to distance themselves from the less powerful, more so when the power distance to the less powerful is larger and less so when it is smaller.

B. Less powerful people are inclined to shorten and bridge the power distance between themselves and the more powerful and they do so to a larger extent when the power distance between them and the more powerful is smaller.

Hence, the first hypothesis concerns a downward tendency while the second one is an upward variant. The second form seems to be the more important.

There is a paradoxical effect hidden in the second variant, especially in case of those who already have a lot, but want more. It seems that by sniffing and tasting it people become addicted to power (or the opportunities for promotion, or the higher salary). Consuming power reinforces the need for power, in a fashion comparable to, in Mulder's words, the effect of the use of hard drugs. It does not matter what has been the cause of the first acquisition of power, whether own achievement or coincidence. Those who are almost at the top, want more. This tendency towards reduction of power distance leads to an almost life-and-death competition among people who are just below the top.

The theory of power distance reduction explains why revolutionary movements rarely originate in the lowest regions of society. As it is, they are usually initiated by the more 'arrived' circles, the circles just below the political and social apex. Admittedly, this is also related to the fact that it is precisely these circles that have the resources (money, weapons, media, etc.) to come into action, in the first place.[17] But the behavioural mechanism, as explained by Mulder, plays an important role in this. Just remember the striking role of Sukarno, a university graduated engineer, who set up the independence movement in the then Dutch East Indies. His academic achievements put him on par with the Dutch elite, but because of his origin, not quite, which explains his political stance. Likewise Mohammed Atta, the leader of the 9/11 hijackers, had all but graduated as an engineer. Dudayev, the leader of the Chechen rebellion, received the rank of Soviet general in 1990, the first Chechen to reach that far in the Soviet military. But being a general is not the same as being a president and hence, he was involved in the burgeoning national movement.[18]

The theory developed by Mulder has many refinements that need not be discussed here. It has been applied in various social settings, ranging from the psychological laboratory to the executive offices and meeting rooms of works councils. But his theory, in complement with the theory of the rising expectations, is also very important for understanding a number of aspects of the conflicts raging in the world. When the (national) centres of power wane, the power of the elite groups, representing separate (regional/ethnic) groups, grows. In the first instance, this almost always happens on its own, automatically so to speak, without the elite groups having to make much effort. Such situations occurred not only in the former Soviet Union and the former Yugoslavia, but also in several African hotbeds. This 'gift' (the fall of dictator Barre, the demise of Tito, the weakening of the communist leadership in the former Soviet Union) fired, quite in accordance with Mulder's theory, a taste for more. As mentioned earlier, in the former Soviet Union the leaders of the Baltic states and several areas in the south (e.g. Chechnya) took the opportunity to still the hunger for power with declarations of independence. In the former Yugoslavia, the hunger for power grew with time. This led to conflicts along ethnic lines at the moment that the increased expectations were thwarted by the actions of other parties, exactly as the theory of rising expectations predicts.

Again, completely in line with Mulder's theory, is a specific type of leadership behaviour in the course of the conflicts. The leaders of the new groups (or clans, small states, or political/religious movements) often care little for the interests and need for participation of their followers and supporters; especially those who have tried the hardest to bridge the power distance with the old centre of power (by destroying it), will attempt to oppose the less powerful, i.e. their subordinates. This is quite in keeping with Mulder's theory (see key hypothesis A, the downward variant of the theory). This phenomenon has been seen quite often in history, which explains the frequently dictatorial behaviour of new leaders (i.e., chiefs of clans, warlords or prime ministers).

One example may suffice to illustrate this. In a newspaper interview, a number of peasants from the mountainous areas of Chechnya had their say. This was shortly after the outbreak of hostilities, in the early 1990s.

They accused their leader in the struggle for independence against Russia, Dudayev, of showing no consideration for them, because of his intention to carry on the war from the mountains. Such mountain warfare would have very negative consequences for the peasants living there. The Russia opponent would see every farm as a potential pocket of resistance and attempt to destroy it. The farmers succinctly expressed their worries and their ensuing irritation, 'It doesn't matter to us which idiot rules us, Yeltsin or Dudayev'.[19]

Notes

1. Horowitz, D.L., op. cit., 123–124, 1985; see also Coleman, J.S., op. cit., 471, 1994. With respect to the often political character of the reproaches against the economic elite, see Chua, A., op. cit., 2003.
2. Elster, J., op. cit., 163, 1993.
3. These patterns can be found in Coleman, J.S., op. cit., Chapter 18, 1994. These ideas have been criticised by Aya, R., *Rethinking Revolutions and Collective Violence. Studies on Concept, Theory and Method*, Het Spinhuis, Amsterdam, 1990. This criticism is valid insofar as it stresses the need for conceptual and empirical improvements. The author's conclusion that social scientists should refrain from pattern finding like this and should stick to the analysis of separate cases only, however, is going backward instead of going forward.
4. van Doorn, J.A.A. and Hendrix, W.J., op. cit., 30, 1970.
5. Arts, W., op. cit., 1996.
6. Tishkov, V., op. cit., 57 and 66, 2004.
7. Stouffer, S.A. *et al.*, *The American Soldier*, Vol I and II, Princeton UP, Princeton, 1949. See also Coleman, J.S., op. cit., 476, 1994.
8. Coleman, J.S., op. cit., 476–477, 1994.
9. Tishkov, V., op. cit., 53 and 67, 2004.
10. Chua, A., op. cit., 2003.
11. Information provided by Nives Elez, who is a Croatian interpreter to the Dutch SFOR troops in Split.
12. This classical text is from Davies, J.C., Toward a theory of revolution, *American Sociological Review*, 27, 5–19, 1962, the quotation is on page 6. See also Lopreato, J., Authority relations and class conflict, in Lopreato, J. and Lewis, L. (eds.), *Social Stratification: a Reader*, Harper and Row, New York, 7–16, 1974; Gurr, T.R., *Why Men Rebel*, Princeton University Press, Princeton, 1970.
13. A description of the tumultuous developments in the former Yugoslavia can, for instance, be found in Gagnon, V.P. Jr., op. cit., 1994.
14. de Temmerman, E., op. cit., 247ff, 1994. See also Broch-Due, V. (ed.), op. cit., 2005, especially Chapter 10 authored by Johan Pottier.
15. Mulder, M., *Het spel om de macht. Over vergroting en verkleining van machtongelijkheid (The Power Game. On the Enlargement and Reduction of Power Inequality)*, Boom, Meppel, 1978; see also Extra, J., *Mulder en de klassenstrijd* (Mulder and the class struggle), in Wiegman, O. and

Wilke, H.A.M. (eds.), *Macht en beïnvloeding (Power and Influence)*, Van Loghum Slaterus, Deventer, 69–79, 1987. In a critical analysis of Mulder's work, Extra has shown that the upward tendency to power distance reduction has been demonstrated more convincingly than the downward directed tendency to enlarge power distance, see Extra, J., *De machtsafstandsreductie— theorie van Mulder* (Mulder's power distance reduction theory), *Nederlands Tijdschrift voor de Psychologie,* 33, 305–320, 1978.

16. Elster, J., op. cit., 64, 1993.
17. Aya, R., op. cit., 58, 1990.
18. Tishkov, V., op. cit., 59, 2004.
19. *Volkskrant*, 20 January 1995.

10

THE DYNAMICS OF CONFLICT

A final factor on the micro level concerns the 'course' of conflicts and acts of violence. People and parties embark on something (e.g. the pursuit of independence of Croatia or the Basque Province, a hate campaign against the Tutsis in Rwanda, the recognition of indigenous languages in Bolivia) without having the slightest idea what this will lead to. But people do not support the ambitions and objectives of leaders just like that. Usually, the recruitment of supporters of a new movement goes through a certain development over time. This development is linked to the psychological, social and possibly, economic profits of participation in the movement.

A minority begins with it and enjoys, if the mission is only the slightest bit successful, a certain hero's role as political forerunners, entrepreneurs or trendsetters. That is the provisional reward for their efforts. But the majority of the population waits and watches which way the wind blows and does not embrace the new political endeavour. For the time being, they prefer the *status quo*, chiefly because they feel safe and comfortable in their large numbers. This is their psychological and social reward.

The average profit of those who advocate the new mission (independence, etc.) subsequently decreases, in proportion to the increase in their numbers. After all, they become less special, with their exclusiveness thinning and the novelty wearing off. This is the moment when the new movement may stagnate. The difference between the psychological and social profits for the minority with the new mission, and the conventional majority increases. The only way to prevent stagnation of the new movement is to increase the efforts in one way or the other, in order to convince the 'ordinary people' in the conventional majority to switch camp.

Especially the original leaders of the new mission may cause these efforts to take the guise of intensive political (and, for instance, also religious) propaganda, tough action and violence. The leaders and followers of the new mission will start to exert some violence — fighting, looting, arson — and people will be compelled to watch this.[1] This will make it harder to stay in the conventional camp. Hesitation and doubt will increase and the comfortable 'feeling of togetherness' will gradually ebb away.

If, in that case, the movement does not stagnate, the psychological and social profits of belonging to the conventional majority decrease in proportion to the minority's increase in numbers. This decrease of profits will become stronger when the new movement is almost the same in numbers as the conventional 'party'.

Somewhere beyond the fifty-fifty mark, there is a tipping point at which participation in the movement with the new mission yields more psychological and social profits than in the original conventional majority. The gain of the original minority is the loss of the original majority. There are three factors at play in reaching the tipping point:

- The special character of the forerunners (both at the level of the 'visionaries' and at the level of the 'riot captains')
- The appeal and power of the message (as in commercials, where some messages stick better than others; as mentioned before, myths and stories, but particularly rumours about events that may or may not have occurred, play a significant role in the origin of conflicts)[2]
- The context of the situation (culture, economic circumstances)[3]

In fact, they are factors that have been discussed before; the charisma of the leaders or forerunners, the nature and persuasiveness of stereotypes, ideologies and enemy images and macro factors, such as culture, inclination to violence, quality of public administration, economic effects of globalisation, etc.

Figure 9 represents the course described above. Of course, this process can also take a different course. The figure is only intended to illustrate the dynamics of the recruitment of supporters of new social or political 'missions'. Nevertheless, the pattern sketched here is a relatively general one. It can be applied in explaining the success of numerous new political movements (e.g. the velvet revolutions of 1989, the violence in Rwanda in 1994, the street protests in Belgrade and Sofia of 1996–1997 and Osama Bin Laden's 'success' in a country like Pakistan). But this course can also regularly be discerned outside the world of politics and conflict. For instance, in the world of fashion, the adoption of new styles often follows the same pattern; and epidemics, too, develop along these lines.

Thus, a change from 'old' to 'new' takes place in politics. Of course, this does not always have to lead to violence and conflict. In some cases it does, though, particularly because people lack sufficient analytical ability and their decision making in such circumstances is poor.

Analysis and decision making

In complex situations, such as during political upheaval, the normal thinking patterns of people, known as 'spontaneous thinking', is often inadequate.[4]

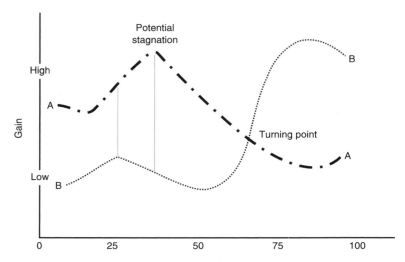

Figure 9 Course of recruitment processes for new political 'missions' (A is old politics; B is new politics). Source: Based on Laitin, D.D., National revivals and violence, *European Journal of Sociology*, 16–18, 1995.

These shortcomings relate to a great number of things. People have the tendency to think in simple causal chains, with only a few steps ahead at best. Events, however, usually occur with the dynamics of positive or negative feedback. This reinforces or cancels out the behavioural effects in mutual relations in various degrees of intensity. There is not a single human being capable of fathoming all those interactions in the form of a 'model'. Such limitations in spontaneous thinking explain in general the occurrence of accidents, but violence and conflict are also caused by them. An example of this was given in Chapter 7, in the so-called reception effect. People begin to talk increasingly louder without being aware of what this leads to. Likewise, people allow themselves to be carried away in reinforcing the enemy image without realising where all this will end.

Furthermore, people think in terms of trial and error, the step-by-step elimination of mistakes. Often they just do something, hoping for a positive result. But this way of thinking has more limitations when the complexity and, consequently, the number of causal connections, increases. Moreover, people have a tendency not to recognise the negative consequences of their own actions, or to exaggerate the negative effects of someone else's. This phenomenon is known as the 'attribution error'. When something goes wrong, 'the other is to blame', sooner rather than later. As a result of this process, people often persist for a long time in their own defective behaviour — 'we didn't do anything wrong, did we?' Success, on the other hand, is often attributed to one's own actions and this is done by almost everyone, which is why 'success knows many fathers' and 'failures are orphans'.

Besides, people are not easily persuaded to change their idea of reality when faced with failures or indications to the contrary. Often they would sooner change their perception of reality than their own ideas and 'practical theories', as is explained in the doctrine of the 'reduction of cognitive dissonance'. When a platoon commander, for instance, is convinced that homosexuals can never be good soldiers and he subsequently finds out that one of his men, who functions well, is a homosexual, he will probably do one of two things. He will, on second thoughts, think his subordinate is not that good, or he will convince himself that this gay guy must be an exception to the rule. The theory of the reduction of cognitive dissonance shows that people do not soon abandon their original ideas. Rather, the reality, in their perception, is adapted a bit. Finally, people do not like 'cynical causalities'. That is why they find it hard to contemplate that 'good' intentions may have 'bad' consequences.[5]

An example of all these shortcomings of spontaneous thinking concerns the 'blind' arms race between two parties, as can also be seen in several internal conflicts. Both parties take their own 'good' intentions for granted and consider their own armament to be defensive, and that of the opponent as aggressive. This is an example of an attribution error. The possibility that one's own good intentions may have bad consequences is ignored and there is insufficient awareness that both parties are actively contributing to an escalation (cynical, step-by-step thinking). Furthermore, the fact that arms races have, for a long time, been unsuccessful is ignored (cognitive dissonance). Given all these limitations, the parties are just messing about a bit (trial and error). After all, the structure of the interactions is complex and therefore future developments are hard to predict.[6]

A related danger is the so-called 'non-rational escalation of involvement'. This problem occurs in far reaching, large-scale decisions. Once a decision has been taken, it often happens that people cannot deviate from it, even if there are indications that the chosen course is the wrong one. After all, giving in to these signals would imply incompetence. An urge for internal and external justification often makes people persevere in their original choices. Nobody wants to be known as a loser. The fear of such a loss of authority and reputation is usually high among decision makers.[7]

The consequence is that they get entangled, as it were, in a fatal situation, from which there is no escape. This phenomenon can also regularly be observed outside the sphere of violence and conflict, for instance, in the selection of investment and project plans. In conflict situations and elsewhere, escalating involvement can land one knee-deep in the big muddy.[8] The account of the Vietnam War is a classic example, as the memoirs of Robert McNamara, the then US Secretary of Defense, makes it all too plain.[9]

This process of no return is very likely playing a significant role in many of today's conflicts.

On top of all this, important decisions in conflict situations are also often subject to so-called 'groupthink', which renders optimism about the rational content of decisions with regard to violence and conflict totally out of place. Groupthink implies that under pressure of circumstances, people look up to the leader too much, alternatives are not seriously considered and an atmosphere of boundless optimism prevails. Under the influence of groupthink, everyone looks too much in one and the same direction, which is an important recipe for the origin and escalation of violence.[10]

Limitations to the cognitive capabilities of people are aggravated under the pressure of external circumstances, such as the lack of sleep or time, the influence of emotions such as envy, shame, frustration and the urge to retaliate. Shame is often a reaction to humiliation and especially when that shame is not recognised by those involved, there is a great chance of discordant behaviour, rage, aggression and an urge to retaliate. When the feeling of humiliation ('Mad Mullah') and the ensuing shame is never recognised by the person who is humiliated and never discussed (with the other party, the party carrying out the humiliation), these feelings remain subdued, only to erupt at the slightest provocation.[11] The urge to retaliate is an important, almost addictive element in the development of conflicts. It almost takes possession of you, as President Eisenhower once put it.[12] Finally, there is the factor of callousness.[13] In fact, this is all about lack of emotions. Having once chosen the path of violence, there is no way back, neither legally, for the difference in punishment for three or thirty murders is limited, nor psychologically or socially, for once a murderer, always a murderer, for yourself as well as for others. For this reason alone, violence begets other violence.

Human, 'all too human' factors influence the quality of the decision making and the course of conflicts in a negative way. It is clear that such phenomena have affected the course of the conflicts in the former Yugoslavia, Rwanda and all the other hotbeds, such as Sierra Leone, the Sudan, Liberia, Sri Lanka, Northern Ireland and the Basque province. In a confluence of drastic events, involving several parties and multiple sets of rules, nobody can foresee the final outcome. Given the shortcomings of 'spontaneous thinking' and the human limitations relating to emotions (or the lack thereof), everyone seems caught up in the vicious circles of events.

Game theory

It seems that the game theory that concerns itself with the processes described above has devised practical recipes for acting in certain situations. Political scientist Robert Axelrod describes which behaviour gives the best chance of success (or survival, if you please) in game situations of the so-called prisoner's dilemma type.[14] These are situations in which parties are condemned to each other for a longer period of time. The dilemma is 'to concede too little or too much', where 'one does the former out of fear of doing the latter'.[15]

Computer simulations clearly showed that in this sort of situations 'do as you would be done by' works best. Even if the starting point is an emphatic self-interest and the other party is anything but a friendly power, it is still important to embark on the game situation with a disposition directed at collaboration. One should not be envious or exclusively bent on thwarting the success of the other party. But that is only one side and the beginning of the story. Subsequently, one only needs to repeat the 'moves' of the other party (in a positive or negative sense), in order to reach the optimum game result for both parties. This implies, however, that one has to be able to hit back in the same manner as the other party. This strategy, therefore, has two elements:

A) 'Being nice, that is to say, never being the first to defect'
B) 'Do what the other player did on the previous move'[16]

This tit-for-tat approach — a) be directed at collaboration, but b) if necessary, react directly — seems to work.

When both parties, out of distrust or self-interest, only show behaviour that is not directed at collaboration, the final outcome is disastrous. For both parties, the result will be much worse than if they had collaborated. Destruction and self-destruction then go hand in hand. When, on the other hand, one of the parties is exclusively and continuously positive and the other is not, the final outcome is completely unbalanced and at the expense of the former that is constantly being deceived or punished. This is known as the 'sucker's alternative', as all 'gain' goes to the other party.

This situation resembles the somewhat disheartening interaction between UN personnel and Serb militias in Bosnia at the time of the UNPROFOR mission there (1991–1995). The UN soldiers were not allowed or were powerless to do anything, which gave the Serbs the opportunity to do whatever they wanted. The UN ended up with the 'sucker's alternative'. A comparable situation occurred in Rwanda as a result of an inadequate UN mandate that rendered the Belgian UN contingent there incapable of staging corrective or even protective action.[17] That such UN action would not be very successful could already have been deduced from empirical research into the effectiveness of hundreds of UN operations. In general, it showed that UN operations are more successful when their legitimacy is broader and when there is a possibility to use (or threaten with) force, if necessary. UN operations on a limited mandate and exclusively equipped for patrolling and observation, generally speaking, do not prove very successful in terms of conflict solution.[18]

Military operations, also those of the UN, must always be able to do 'what the other player did on the previous move'. That is the bitter lesson that had to be learned in the tough practice of UN operations in the 1990s. It was learned surprisingly late in the day; Axelrod had published his theory ten years before. If the Dutch soldiers in Srebrenica had had at their disposal a number of heavy tanks and other heavy equipment (to be able to do what 'the other party did on the previous move'), thousands of victims might have been saved. However, against the insights the theory had furnished, the Dutch government decided not to send such heavy armoury along. It is also possible that they did not know the theory.

But the theory has not been fully explained yet. There is a third rule to make it complete. As mentioned above, investing in mutual trust and collaboration can have a de-escalating effect, or even prevent the flaring up of conflict. This is the first rule of the theory ('never be the first to defect') and it should be the guiding principle in determining tactics that involve violence. Apart from that, the tit-for-tat approach includes the possibility to hit back ('do what the other player did on the previous move'). This is the second rule. But this part of the theory carries a certain risk of escalation, as could be seen in the arms race during the Cold War. Also, the many ethnic conflicts of today illustrate the limitations of the second rule. In order to prevent escalation, it is often wise not to give tit-for-tat immediately. It can be decided not to do it until the second 'offence' has occurred, or to only partially retaliate against the violence of the opponent (for 90%, for instance). So, there is a reaction on the violence of the opponent, but only after some time (during which warnings can be given), or it is somewhat less intense. Tit-for-tat works, but it works even better when it contains elements of forgiveness, and this is the third rule of the theory.[19]

Apart from this, there are still other ways of increasing the chances of mutual trust and collaboration with the opponent. In the first place, it is important to aim for realistic, attainable goals in conflicts. When they are not, there is every chance that the conflicts will drag on indefinitely. Furthermore, institutionalised conflicts, with rules of behaviour based on mutual recognition, are relatively less bloody and violent. There may be awareness in this that it is better to not fully destroy each other, so that the opponent does not have to make very great sacrifices. In doing so, the chance of depletion of one's own ranks is also diminished. Or perhaps, there is a realisation that at a later stage there may be possibilities for collaboration on points other than the disputed ones. A further argument is that 'decently' fought out conflicts lower the need to retaliate against the opponent. Who decides a conflict with blood, often creates the conditions for the outbreak of a new conflict. Who, on the other hand, exercises self-restraint and makes some (symbolic) gestures, at least attempts to try for reconciliation. An example is of the Thai dropping millions of paper Origami birds above the Muslim provinces in the South where so many protesters had died in 2004.[20]

But sober considerations like these, leading to mutual trust and a readiness to collaborate between the various parties, are often far away in the conflicts and areas of tensions. That is why it should always be taken into account that violence in these situations may always flare up again and escalate as a consequence of the dynamics of the conflict itself.

Notes

1. Horowitz, D.L., op. cit., 71ff, 2001.
2. About the role of rumours, see Horowitz, D.L., op. cit., Chapter 3, 2001. In Mitrovica, an ethnically divided city in Kosovo (North: Serbian; South: Albanian), large-scale deathly violence broke out when Albanian newspapers reported about the alleged killing of three Albanian children by a number of Serbian children. The UN authorities in the region called these reports premature and in fact irresponsible, because there had been no certainty up to that moment about the actual course of events. But the damage was done. In the battle, more than 300 people were wounded (among them 11 KFOR military) and some 10 persons died. See Tempelman, O., *Veldslag in etnisch verdeelde stad in Kosovo* (Battle in ethnically divided city in Kosovo), *Volkskrant*, 18 March 2004.
3. Gladwell, M., *The Tipping Point. How Little Things Can Make a Big Difference*, Little, Brown and Cy., Boston, 2000.
4. Masuch, M., op. cit., 1985.
5. Masuch, M., op. cit., especially pages 450–451, 1985. A comparable, more extensive survey of these social-psychological mechanisms can be found in Kelman, H.C., Social-psychological dimensions of international conflict, in William Zartman, I. and Lewis Rasmussen J., (eds.), *Peacemaking in International Conflict. Methods & Techniques*, United States Institute of Peace, Washington DC, 191–237, 2001.
6. This example, concerning the arms race between two parties is also given by Masuch, M., op. cit., 451, 1985.
7. Flam, H., op. cit., especially pages 70–71, 1994.
8. Staw, B.M., Knee-deep in the big muddy: a study of escalating commitment to a chosen course of action, *Organizational Behavior and Human Performance*, 16, 27–44, 1976.
9. McNamara, R.S., *In Retrospect. The Tragedy and Lessons of Vietnam*, Times Books, New York, 1995.
10. Hart, P.T., *Groepsdenken in cruciale beslissingen; collectieve vermijding en overoptimisme* (Groupthink in crucial decision making; collective avoidance and overoptimism), *Psychologie en Maatschappij*, 14, 226–241, 1990.
11. Th.J. Scheff, *Bloody Revenge. Emotions, Nationalism and War*, iUniverse, Lincoln, 2000; see also Zwaan, T., op. cit., 353–354, 2001.

12. See for descriptions of this phenomenon occurring during the police actions in the then Dutch East Indies, van Doorn, J.A.A. and Hendrix, W.J., op. cit., 108, 1970.
13. Laitin, D.D., op. cit., 1995.
14. Axelrod, R., *The Evolution of Cooperation*, Basic Books, New York, especially Chapter 2, 1984.
15. Elster, J., op. cit., 163, 1993.
16. Axelrod, R., op. cit., 1984; quotations are on pages 31 and 33.
17. de Temmerman, E., op. cit., 1994. See, for instance, the vicissitudes of Zambian UN soldiers witnessing a brutal act of retaliation by Tutsi military on Hutu citizens. The citizens were locked in a refugee camp and could not go anywhere. The NGO personnel, who happened to be on the spot, criticised the Zambians for not intervening. But they in turn referred to the inadequate UN mandate that made them watch the events without being able to interfere. See also de Temmerman, E., *Zij hebben de vluchtelingen ginds laten rotten* (They let the refugees get rotten over there), *Volkskrant*, 26 April 1995.
18. Segal, D.R. and Waldman, R.J., Multinational peacekeeping operations: background and effectiveness, in Burk, J., *The Military in New Times*, Westview Press, Boulder, 1994.
19. Axelrod, R., op. cit., especially 39 and 138, 1984; see also Chapter 7.
20. Teitler, G., op. cit., 19, 1972. See also Coser, L.A., The termination of conflict, *Journal of Conflict Resolution*, 5, 347–353, 1961; and more extensively in Deutsch, M., *The Resolution of Conflict*, Yale University Press, New Haven, especially Chapter 13, 1973. See also Axelrod, R., op. cit., chapter 7, 1984. 'The dropping of Thai paper birds' is reported in Anonymous, *Thailand paait moslims met origami-vogels* (Thailand appeases Muslims with Origami-birds), *Volkskrant*, 6 December 2004.

11

CONCLUSIONS AND IMPLICATIONS

The preceding pages have presented a survey of the factors that cause the occurrence of conflict and violence. A distinction has been made between macro and micro factors. The former category constitutes the fertile (or not so fertile) breeding ground for violence, the latter concerns the concrete interactions between the people who cause the actual violence. When attempting to explain specific expressions of violence, macro and micro factors always constitute a unique combination of influences that only applies to that particular place and time. This combination determines the conditions, causes, occasions and characteristics of the development of a conflict. The general picture that emerges from the above is represented schematically in Figure 10.

Violence seems to be especially rife in societies that have not yet fully modernised. They are pre-eminently societies that are engaged in a process of change or turmoil. In the words of one of the founders of sociology, Emile Durkheim, they are societies that are on their way from a traditional society, based on mechanical solidarity, to a modern society, based on organic solidarity.[1] In the modern, organic society, division of labour has progressed far and the population has become strongly heterogeneous due to urbanisation, increased mobility and migration. Whereas in traditional communities people are the same everywhere and act the same (pious farmers), in modern society, the differences between people are dominant. The Catholic lives beside the Protestant, black beside white, guest worker beside migrant labourer, service provider beside production worker, the 'white' collar beside the 'blue' collar. All this is not a problem, since in the organic society, all 'pieces' of the societal puzzle (institutions, communities, etc.) fit in with each other.

All people contribute in an organic, i.e. harmonious, manner to the total functioning of the community. Like a body that needs all organs to function as a whole, society too needs all these different kinds of people to function fully. Besides, people are convinced that they can make a useful contribution to the greater whole, for the societal rules, values and norms are completely tuned in to the structure of society and the division of labour.

119

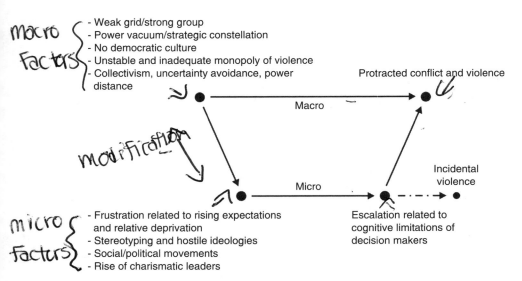

Figure 10 Survey of factors on macro and micro level that cause violence and conflict to occur. Based on Coleman, J.S., *Foundations of Social Theory*, Belknap Press, Cambridge, MA, 10 and 478, 1994.

Nobody is, but also nobody feels discriminated against, at least in the Durkheimian ideal type of the modern society.

But precisely in the changeover to that organic society, the various social elements have not found their place yet and are not well adapted to each other. There are imbalances in rights and duties, rewards and punishments, freedoms and limitations, opportunities and rules. Certain groups are excluded from participating in social processes or only get an unequal share of the benefits of prosperity and social progress. It is not only the imbalances themselves that matter here. They could be acceptable and legitimised by an undisputed culture, stable power relations and confidence-inspiring institutions. But when these elements — a legitimising culture and stable power relations and institutions — are absent, the influence of the imbalances really becomes manifest. Not only the objective imbalances, but especially the significance attached to them is relevant for the emergence of satisfaction deficits.

Imbalances that are not, or no longer, legitimised in the changeover to a modern, heterogeneous and organic society lead to confusion and a lack of norms, with all the ensuing negative consequences. Such a situation often causes the emergence of emotional, often irrational and highly contagious ideas that spread from one category of the population to the next, from one individual to the next. The changeover or transition process, not the starting point or the goal, leads to dissatisfaction and frustration, which in their turn

120

spawn feelings of discrimination, superstition, despair, rivalry, jealousy, rage, indifference, hatred and eventually also conflict and violence, not only towards others, but also towards oneself. In such periods of transition, people often have no alternative but suicide. In sociology this is known as *suicide anomique*, a variant of the *suicide altruiste* described in Chapter 8 in the discussion on suicide terrorists. In the former Soviet Union, there is a true suicide epidemic among people who are desperate after the fall of the communist regime.[2] In the Netherlands, the number of suicides among farmers is staggeringly high, for the simple reason that the agricultural sector is going through dramatic changes and the life of a farmer will never again be as it was in the past.

The havoc such a changeover process can wreak on a community is best illustrated by the story of the Iks people.[3] The Iks were a small hunting tribe in northern Uganda. On the authority of the government, they had to leave their territory for a national park that was going to be established there. The Iks were forced to give up their nomadic existence and to begin to farm the land in a barren area. An anthropologist lived among them in this new environment for two years. His record is a shocking account of the indifferent, callous way in which the Iks treated each other. They never co-operated, shared nothing, but only jeered at each other, especially when they had relieved themselves on another's doorstep. It was a mean, cold society. The changeover had turned them into cruel, indifferent people. As it happened, there were no other groups living in the same area on which the Iks could give full rein to their frustration. Besides, they felt powerless in the face of their government. But it is clear that the cruelty and hatred, which was directed at their own people, could easily turn into violence towards other groups in different circumstances.

One of these circumstances is the availability of (modern) means of violence. This is an important fact. Even relatively limited conflicts emanate a major threat due to the almost unrestricted availability of lethal weapons, ranging from the traditional (machetes) to the more contemporary ones (mines, explosives, nerve agents and of course, AK-47 'Kalashnikovs'). The leaders of the movements in general make sure that their followers have the means to start the killing. Months before the atrocities in Rwanda began, tens of thousands of machetes were imported from the People's Republic of China.[4] No less important is the role of the media, the radio stations, the newspapers and currently also the Internet. In all conflicts, from Rwanda to Bosnia, the 'hate stations' and the nationalist papers play their outrageously inciting role.[5] When one reads the story of the role of the media in these countries, it is not in the least surprising that the people in the former Yugoslavia who read many papers, were less tolerant that those who read (almost) none.[6] Particularly in countries that are (still) unbalanced, such modern means can apparently have considerably contrary effects.

The above description is particularly applicable to what Singer and Wildavsky call the 'zones of turmoil' or the 'chaos areas'. They are areas — and they take up large parts of the world — with a considerable chance of violent conflicts breaking out between, but especially within, countries. Writers such as Huntington and van Creveld draw a lot of attention to this message in their captivating observations. Their books already enjoyed great popularity among a large public and politicians, and since 9/11 they have certainly not lost their importance. But even if their assertions are occasionally somewhat too bold, the essence of their message remains intact, and that is the warning of the threat of violent conflicts in large parts of the world.[7]

But, however justified it may be to draw attention to these areas, the modernised, Western societies, too, find themselves in a changeover phase; perhaps, even again. Several countries in Northwest Europe, it could be argued, may have attained a situation of 'organic solidarity' in the 1950s or 1960s, but the following decades brought it to a rather abrupt end. Since those days, the world economy has been re-shuffling — low-wage countries emerged, new technologies made the division of labour even more international than it was already and there is the threat of scarcity of natural resources.

The effect of all this is that Western countries, too, are threatened by a certain disruption through mass unemployment caused by the transfer of work elsewhere and the arrival of new employees who accept lower pay, through the increase of the number of people of foreign origin, through social exclusion of large groups of people and the erosion of social relations (education, family, church, association).[8] As, in particular, the example of the United States shows, this macro phenomenon can lead to an unprecedented extent of violence on the micro level through the emergence of cultures of violence. It has been pointed out before that, in terms of numbers, crime in American cities is comparable to what has emerged in Bosnia. With regard to size and bloodshed, the racial riots in Los Angeles are often not so different from several incidents in the former Yugoslavia. The United States also knows the phenomenon of 'hate stations' that in no uncertain terms preach violent resistance against the government.[9]

Add to this the possible 'radiation' of foreign conflicts to Western countries and it becomes clear that these countries are definitely not immune to a possible increase in violence. Consider, for example, the import of violent crime from the former Yugoslavia, i.e. crime syndicates in Western Europe who hire experienced, callous ex-fighters from the Bosnian war to do the 'dirty jobs'. Finally, there is the migration pressure from developing countries that shows that the prosperous West does not live in 'splendid isolation'. The thriving West and the rest of the world are increasingly interdependent, as was seen above; as a consequence, the West is no longer immune to the problems that occur elsewhere.[10]

In Singer and Wildavsky's analysis, Western countries are 'zones of peace'; this qualification is justified when it concerns the slight chance that these fully grown democracies will ever wage war against each other again. But that does not take away the possibility of extensive violence within these zones of peace. As Mary Kaldor puts it, 'the world is no longer divided in zones of war and zones of peace'.[11] This is a bit exaggerated and incomprehensible for those who have to go through a personal experience of civil wars, deportations and genocide, but this statement does indicate the direction in which the world is moving. Violence, terror and conflict are becoming increasingly widespread. This is what people know in New York and Washington, in Bali, Riyadh, Moscow and since March 2004, also in Madrid.

Implications and considerations

This conclusion begs further reflection on the possibilities to curb this threat of violence. An inventory of factors that cause violence, as has been attempted above, unfortunately does not lead to a number of practical guidelines with regard to the question of how to avert or end conflict. In general, one should not be too optimistic about preventing or ending conflicts. Conflicts can stop in three ways — suppression of one party by the other, separation of the conflicting parties or some form of integration and reconciliation, the latter of course being the preferred, peaceful solution.[12] But even in this case, it proves difficult for people to live together after serious hostilities have taken place, as the harrowing novel *Homecoming* by the Bosnian writer Natasha Radojčič convincingly demonstrates.[13]

But despite this pessimistic tone, the factors culminating in violent conflict that we have seen in this book may provide some ideas to avert, curb or end it. The following, non-exhaustive ideas and considerations, i.e. implications of the insights presented before, can be mentioned.

1. In order to prevent and avert the various 'regional' conflicts in the world a supranational co-ordination of policy seems necessary. This is what is attempted by the UN and other institutions such as the Organization for African Unity, the European Union and Mercosur, the counterpart of the EU in Latin America. Such supranational institutions stress co-ordination, collaboration and interdependence instead of competition, rivalry and conflict. But there is quite something to be said against the UN, in particular, in its role as violence monopolist and maintainer of law and order. First and foremost, nation states will pursue their own interests and in doing so, will often hinder effective combined action. As a result, there is a lot of scepticism and criticism of the UN and other international institutions at the moment. The most extreme example of this is the Bush administration, which could not wait for UN approval

to invade Iraq in the spring of 2003. It is because of this attitude of some countries that the UN and similar institutions are all too easily seen as powerless.[14] But that does not mean that there is a reason to quit these attempts at an international co-ordination of policy. On the contrary, a 'community of communities', as sociologist Etzioni calls it, is necessary to stand guard over each other, as it were.[15]

2. A reinforcement of the UN is unavoidable for the resolution of the many regional conflicts in the world and it can be realised in various ways. In the first place, there is the plea to empower the UN Security Council to interfere in internal conflicts. In addition, it is necessary to reinforce the international maintenance of law and order by the UN. This function has considerably improved over the past years due to the establishment of international criminal tribunals (Yugoslavia, Rwanda and the International Criminal Tribunal) and the development will have to be continued. Apart from this, there is the idea of rigging up UN military units, not with the intent of replacing national units, but to offer a sort of 'first military resort'. These units would have to be established on the basis of the well-understood self-interest of the participating countries. There should be a growing awareness that the attainment of peace and stability in the world is a collective good for the benefit of all. The establishment of these military units would have to take place on the principles of the same well-understood self-interest that in the past, instigated regions and cities to create nation states and their armies. Such supranational military forces would crown the process of up-scaling and increasing civilisation described by Elias. It would be a step towards the pacification of the world.[16]

3. Parallel to the necessity to reinforce the supranational co-ordination of policy, there is a development that is already in progress, namely a development of and for citizens anywhere in the world. As early as the days of the Abolitionists in the early nineteenth century, something began to emerge that could be called worldwide identification, international solidarity, if you please, with people elsewhere on the globe. Apparently something like a 'human sensitivity' of truly global proportions came into being in those days. This process of international solidarity, of widening circles of identification,[17] has continued since then. There are indications that this development has gained momentum over the past few years. Due to an increasing globalisation combined with advancing communication possibilities via the Internet, many people seem to be organising themselves on a global scale. Their intention is to stand up for the victims of unequal authority relations, violence and conflict. A good example of this phenomenon is the anti-landmine campaign, instigated by citizens, which has become so powerful that its initiator, Jody Williams, was awarded the Nobel Prize for Peace in 1997. What is more important, however, is that this

movement has been instrumental in the creation of a treaty against the proliferation of landmines, which was signed in 1997 by over 140 countries (but not the United States). But this is not the only movement of importance in this connection. There are more citizens' initiatives, sometimes joined by celebrities like the late Princess Diana as well as pop stars like Bono and Youssou N'Dour. These actions can be very influential, not least because of a mobilised public opinion. Also, the Non-Governmental Organisations (NGOs), such as Human Rights Watch and Amnesty International have gradually gained great influence on the world stage. All these activities can be gathered together under the common denominator of 'global civil society' and they are expressions of the pursuit of preventive democracy. Sometimes the actions and proposals have a whiff of utopia about them (such as the proposal to write a 'Declaration of Mutual Dependency'), but it has happened before that utopian ideas later became realities. These movements have only words for 'weapons', but that can be important enough.[18] Finally, in these movements, women play an important role; perhaps this is an indication of the truth of the supposition that if women are given administrative authority, the chance of violence and conflict will decrease globally. Perhaps it is no coincidence that, in addition to Jody Williams in 1997, the Nobel Prize for Peace in 2003 and 2004 was awarded to two more women, namely Shirin Ebadi from Iran and Wangari Mathaai from Kenya, respectively.[19]

4. On the level of the conflicts themselves, the military actions as such are important. They can prevent conflicts and violence, as they did in Macedonia. They can terminate violent conflicts, as eventually happened in the former Yugoslavia, East Timor, Liberia, etc. A thorough quantitative study has demonstrated that international military intervention, preferably at an early stage, really contributes to peace building.[20] Also, bearing in mind the recent troop reductions in Bosnia (from 60,000 to less than 6,000 in 10 years), it is clear that military interventions can be really effective.[21] When the targets have been reached, as in Bosnia, the military can leave, which was the exact intention. So it does work. Military interventions have the best chance of success when there is a mandate and equipment that is taken seriously. They should not be condemned to the sucker's alternative, as was so often the case in the early 1990s. At the same time, the chance of escalation must be minimal, for the possibility of the conflict flaring up again is always there. For some parties the presence of foreign troops remains a source of much irritation, as is still the case in Kosovo.

5. The risk of escalation can be minimised by constantly keeping communication open with all parties. Communication and negotiation skills should therefore be an integral part of the standard military skills of every soldier. Another way to reduce the chance of escalation

is by not immediately giving in to tit-for-tat but to follow the guidelines described earlier in this book. In the post-conflict period, the military must be given an adequate legal mandate in order to effectuate a restoration of public order and a credible maintenance of the law, so that war criminals can indeed be punished.[22] Furthermore, soldiers must be equipped for nation building in the broad sense of the word. They have to be able to contribute, in co-operation with local authorities, NGOs and other parties, to the building of a well-functioning society, including the restoration of human rights.[23] All in all, task conception and equipment of the military must not be too limited.

6. The best way to prevent regional conflicts is to enhance the economic and social development of the areas 'at risk'.[24] After all, virtually every conflict has a background of economic and social disruption. This should work in more than one way. Simultaneous with industrialisation and an acceptation in the global economy, these areas should be developed further with respect to their social, political and legal systems. An adequately functioning democratic, administrative and legal system with an effective violence monopoly is essential in the prevention of those conflicts. The result will be a stronger grid system, which can mitigate the effect of group oppositions, including the systematic neglect of minority groups. At the same time the culture of an area or country will change as the level of prosperity and civilisation increases. A culture of ingroup collectivism is likely to develop into a culture with lesser group pressures and more freedom for the individual person. All these elements subdue the inclination for war and attack. In order to avoid too great an appeal on the 'curative' employment of military means, it is of great importance to operate in a preventive manner, through bilateral development aid, as well as through an adequate global development policy, directed at fair trade relations, education and emancipation of women. Not only does such a policy prevent and limit the outbreak of violent conflicts in these areas, Western countries themselves will also profit. Where there are no violent conflicts, no effects can seep through to the 'safe havens' in the West. Just like the establishment of UN units, the pursuit of an international development policy is a matter of well-understood self interest.[25] A consequence of such a policy is that countries will become economically and militarily entwined (Turkey is not only a NATO member, but also a future EU member, for instance). This is undoubtedly one of the best remedies against the emergence of violence and conflict, even if those conflicts have, strictly speaking, an internal character. Similarly, military, but especially also economic, processes of unification in other continents such as Africa and South America should be stimulated. The European unification shows how countries that previously lived in the greatest possible enmity with each

126

other have become close again in merely a few decades. Such a development should offer hope to the rest of the world.

7. If the peace in Western countries is threatened by heavy crime and the responsible 'violence monopolists' (police, the legal system) fail in the eyes of the citizens, violence may increase. Then 'decent citizens', at least the more aggressive among them, will take matters into their own hands. This can also happen when tensions between communities arise. They can be of a religious nature, as has already been noticed from time to time. But the background can be more trivial; people have had enough of the 'nuisance', or they are envious of the social success of the newcomers, especially when they themselves are in danger of lagging behind socially.[26] These are all scenarios that may lead to social conflicts, even in modernised societies. Possibly, the level of civilisation of the criminal prosecution may drop, when, for instance, the call for the re-introduction of the death penalty becomes louder. The United States has already taken up a leading position with regard to all these developments. Recently, in Alabama, the use of the so-called chain gang was re-introduced. This practice, in which prisoners are chained to each other and have to do forced labour on public roads, had been abolished in 1932. Also, with regard to this matter, it is important that there is a balance between curative and preventive measures. Particularly in the United States, this balance seems to be somewhat disturbed.

8. But European countries also, such as the Netherlands, are not free of risks in this respect. The situation may explode easily. Under pressure, human behaviour can quickly show dangerous, irrational features, as has been seen above, especially when appealing leaders take up the stage. It is these risks that everyone, politicians and citizens alike, should bear in mind.

This brings us to the end of the book. The previous pages have only presented basic analyses and implications, just like this complete survey of the origins of conflict and violence contains only basic, broad outlines. If, however, this survey provides the stimulus for further thought about the bloody and degrading matters that were the catalysts for writing it, then it has reached its objectives.

Notes

1. Durkheim, E., *The Division of Labor in Society*, Free Press, New York, 129ff, 1933.
2. Coleman, J.S., op. cit., 219–220, 1994 on the relations between transition periods and the frequency of so-called 'contagious beliefs'. An account of the suicide epidemic in the former Soviet Union can be found in Alexijevitsj, S., *In de ban van de dood (In Death's Spell)*, Pegasus, Amsterdam, 1995.

3. Turnbull, C.M., *The Mountain People*, Simon and Schuster, New York, 1972.
4. Gourevitch, Ph., op. cit., 104, 1998.
5. de Temmerman, E., op. cit., 1994; Ugresic, D., op. cit., 1995.
6. Hodson, R., Sekulic, D. and Massey, G., op. cit., 1994.
7. Singer, M. and Wildavsky, A., *The Real World Order. Zones of Peace, Zones of Turmoil*, Chatham House Publishers, Chatham, 1993; Huntington, S.P., op. cit., 1996; van Creveld, M., op. cit., 1991.
8. Beck, U., op. cit., Sage, London, 1992.
9. Garschagen, O., *Clinton valt haat-verspreiders aan* (Clinton attacks hate-mongers), *Volkskrant*, 26 April 1995. See also Juergensmeyer, M., op. cit., 2000.
10. de Swaan, A., Perspectives for transnational social policy, *Government and Opposition. A Quarterly of Comparative Politics*, 27, 33–51, 1990.
11. Kaldor, M., *Global Civil Society. An Answer to War*, Polity, Cambridge, 147, 2003.
12. Kaufmann, Ch., op. cit., 1996.
13. Radojčić-Kane, N., *Homecoming*, Four Walls Eight Windows, New York, 2002. For similar, not all too optimistic accounts, see Gourevitch, Ph., op. cit., 1998.
14. See for instance, Mearsheimer, J.J., The false promise of international institutions, *International Security*, 19, 5–49, 1994–95.
15. e.g. Etzioni, A., *The Moral Dimension. Toward a New Economics*, Free Press, New York, 1990.
16. An analysis of Elias' thinking on this subject can be found in St. Mennell, op. cit., 219ff, 1992.
17. de Swaan, A., Widening circles of identification: emotional concerns in sociogenetic perspective, *Theory, Culture and Society*, 12, 25–39, 1995. See also Kymlicka, W., op. cit., 2001.
18. Barber, B., *Fear's Empire. War, Terrorism and Democracy*, Norton, New York, Chapter 9, 2003; Kaldor, M., op. cit., 2003.
19. Adler, N.J., *International Dimensions of Organizational Behavior*, South-Western, Cincinnati, Chapter 10, 2002. For a similar reasoning, see Galtung, J., *Peace by Peaceful Means. Peace and Conflict, Development and Civilization*, Sage, London, Chapter 3, 1996.
20. Doyle, M.W. and Sambanis, N., op. cit., 787–793, 2000. See also Galtung, J., op. cit., 1996, in particular the introduction.
21. Heidenreich, J.G., *How to Prevent Genocide. A Guide for Policy Makers, Scholars, and the Concerned Citizen*, Praeger, Westport, 2001.
22. Kelley, M.J., *Restoring and Maintaining Order in Complex Peace Operations. The Search for a Legal Framework*, Kluwer, The Hague, 1999.
23. Mertus, J., The impact of intervention on local human rights culture: a Kosovo case study, *Global Review of Ethnopolitics*, 1–2, 21–36, 2001.
24. A similar type of reasoning can be found in Tomasic, D., op. cit., 1946 and Hofstede, G.H., op. cit., 1991. The activities of the World Bank constitute an attempt to realise such a worldwide development policy. These activitities, however, do not always go without criticism. According to this criticism, the Bank would make the problems even worse. See George, S. and Sabelli, F.,

Faith and Credit, Penguin, Harmondsworth, 1994; Stiglitz, J., *Globalization and its Discontents*, Norton, New York, 2002.

25. de Swaan, A., op. cit., 1990.
26. In fact this is the scenario that Amy Chua sees as the basic pattern of ethnic violence all over the world; Chua, A., op. cit., 2003.

BIBLIOGRAPHY

Adler, N., *International Dimensions of Organizational Behavior*, South-Western, Cincinnati, 2002.

Ahmed, A., Discovering Islam. *Making Sense of Muslim History and Society*, (rev. ed.), Routledge, London, 2002.

Alexijevitsj, S., *In de ban van de dood (In Death's Spell)*, Pegasus, Amsterdam, 1995.

Allen, B., *Rape Warfare. The Hidden Genocide in Bosnia-Hercegovina and Croatia*, University of Minnesota Press, Minneapolis, 1996.

Aquino Siapno, J., *Gender, Islam, Nationalism and the State in Aceh. The Paradox of Power, Co-optation and Resistance*, RoutledgeCurzon, London, 2002.

Arendt, H., *Eichmann in Jerusalem: a Report on the Banality of Evil*, Faber and Faber, London, 1963.

Armstrong, K., *The Battle for God*, Knopf, New York, 2000.

Arts, W., *Van fluwelen en stille revoluties (Of Velvet and Silent Revolutions)*, Tilburg University Press, Tilburg, 1996.

Axelrod, R., *The Evolution of Cooperation*, Basic Books, New York, 1984.

Aya, R., *Rethinking Revolutions and Collective Violence. Studies on Concept, Theory and Method*, Het Spinhuis, Amsterdam, 1990.

Barber, B., *Fear's Empire. War, Terrorism and Democracy*, Norton, New York, 2003.

Barth, F., (ed.), *Ethnic Groups and Boundaries*, University Press, Oslo, 1969.

Bauer, B. *et al.*, *Le Monde diplomatique. Atlas der Globalisierung*, Berlin, 2003.

Bauman, Z., *Modernity and the Holocaust*, Polity Press, Cambridge, 1991.

Bauman, Z., *Intimations of Postmodernity*, Routledge, London, 1992.

Bax, M., *Medjugorje: Religion, Politics, and Violence in Rural Bosnia*, VU University Press, Amsterdam, 1995.

Beck, I.J., *Risk Society. Toward a New Modernity*, Sage, London, 1986.

Bennett, V., *Crying Wolf. The Return of War to Chechnya*, Pan Books, London, 2001.

Berger, P.L. and Huntington, S.P., (eds.), *Many Globalizations. Cultural Diversity in the Contemporary World*, Oxford UP, Oxford, 2002.

Blok, A., *Honour and Violence*, Polity Press, Cambridge, 2001.

Boon, L., *De list der wetenschap (The Ruse of Science)*, Ambo, Baarn, 1983.

Bovenkerk, F., *Misdaadprofielen (Profiles of Crime)*, Meulenhoff, Amsterdam, 2001.

Brink, G. van den and Schuyt, K., *Van kwaad tot erger. Wordt geweld nu ook gedemocratiseerd? (From bad to worse. Is violence now also being democratized?)*, *Mens en Maatschappij*, 77, 7–17, 2002.

Broch-Due, V., (ed.), *Violence and Belonging. The Quest for Identity in Post-Colonial Africa*, Routledge, London and New York, 2005.

Burk, J., Thinking through the end of the Cold War, in Burk, J., (ed.), *The Military in New Times. Adapting Armed Forces to a Turbulent World*, Westview Press, Boulder, 1–24, 1994.

Burr, J. M. and Collins, R.O., *Requiem for the Sudan – War, Drought and Disaster Relief on the Nile*, Westview Press, Boulder, 1996.

Buruma, I. and Margalit, A., *Occidentalism. The West in the Eyes of its Enemies*, Penguin Press, New York, 2004.

Campbell, G., *Blood Diamonds. Tracing the Deadly Path of the World Most Precious Stones*, Westview Press, Boulder, 2002.

Castells, M., *The Power of Identity*, (sec. edn), Blackwell, Oxford, 2004.

Chua, A., *World on Fire. How Exporting Free Market Democracy Breeds Ethnic Hatred and Global Instability*, Doubleday, New York, 2003.

Cipolla, C.M., (ed.), *The Economic Decline of Empires*, Methuen, London, 1970.

Coakly J., (ed.), *The Territorial Management of Ethnic Conflict*, (sec. and rev. edn), Frank Cass, London, 2003.

Cohen, D., Law, social policy, and violence: the impact of regional cultures, *Journal of Personality and Social Psychology*, 70, 961–978, 1996.

Cohen, D. *et al.*, Insult, aggression, and the Southern culture of honor: an "experimental" ethnography, *Journal of Personality and Social Psychology*, 70, 945–960, 1996.

Coleman, J.S., *Foundations of Social Theory*, Belknap Press, Cambridge, MA 1994.

Collier, P. and Hoeffert, A., On economic causes of civil war, *Oxford Economic Papers*, 50, 563–573, 1998.

Collins, R., Three faces of cruelty: towards a comparative sociology of violence, *Theory and Society*, 1, 415–440, 1974.

Collins, R., On the microfoundations of macrosociology, *American Journal of Sociology*, 86, 984–1014, 1981.

Collins, R., *Weberian Sociological Theory*, Cambridge UP, Cambridge, 1986.

Collins, R., *Gewelddadig conflict en sociale organisatie. Enkele theoretische implicaties van de sociologie van de oorlog* (Violent conflict and social organization. Some theoretical implications of the sociology of war), *Amsterdams Sociologisch Tijdschrift*, 16, 63–87, 1990.

Collins, R., *Four Sociological Traditions. Selected Readings*, Oxford UP, Oxford, 1994.

Collins, R., Prediction in macrosociology: the case of the Soviet collapse, *American Journal of Sociology*, 100, 1552–1593, 1995.

Coser, L.A., The termination of conflict, *Journal of Conflict Resolution*, 5, 347–353, 1961.

Coser, L.A., *Greedy Institutions. Patterns of Undivided Commitment*, Free Press, New York, 1974.

Courtemanche, G., *Een zondag aan het zwembad in Kigali (A Sunday at the Swimming Pool in Kigali)*, De Bezige Bij, Amsterdam, 2003.

van Creveld, M. *The Transformation of War*, Free Press, New York, 1991.

Dahl, G., Will 'the other God' fail again? On the possible return of the conservative revolution, *Theory, Culture and Society*, 13, 25–50, 1996.

Davies, J.C., Toward a theory of revolution, *American Sociological Review*, 27, 5–19, 1962.

Deutsch, K., Cracks in the monolith, in Friedrich, C.J., *Totalitarianism*, Perspective, Cambridge, 308–333, 1954.

Deutsch, M., *The Resolution of Conflict*, Yale University Press, New Haven, 1973.

Dixon, N.F., *The Psychology of Military Incompetence*, Futura, London, 1991.

van Doorn, J.A.A., *Met man en macht. Sociologische studies over maatschappelijke mobilisatie (With Might and Main. Sociological Studies on Societal Mobilization)*, Boom, Meppel, 1973.

van Doorn, J.A.A. and Hendrix, W.J., *Ontsporing van geweld. Over het Nederlands–Indisch–Indonesisch conflict (Derailment of Violence. About the Dutch-Indonesian Conflict)*, Rotterdam UP, Rotterdam, 1970.

Douglas, M., *Natural Symbols. Explorations in Cosmology*, Barrie & Rockliffe, London, 1970; Penguin, London, 1973.

Douglas, M. and Mars, G., Terrorism: a positive feedback game, *Human Relations*, 56, 763–786, 2003.

Doyle, M.W. and Sambanis, N., International peace building: a theoretical and quantitative analysis, *American Political Science Review*, 94, 779–801, 2000.

Duijzings, G., *Geschiedenis en herinnering in Oost-Bosnië (History and Memory in Eastern Bosnia)*, Boom, Amsterdam, 2002.

Dunning, E.G., Murphy, P. and Williams, J., *The Roots of Football Hooliganism: a Historical and Sociological Study*, Routledge, London, 1988.

Durkheim, E., *The Division of Labor in Society*, Free Press, New York and London, 1933.

Eisenstadt, S.N. and Giesen, B., The construction of collective identity, *European Journal of Sociology*, 36, 72–102, 1995.

Elias, N., On transformations of aggressiveness, *Theory and Society*, 5, 219–228, 1978.

Elias, N., *Studien über die Deutschen (Studies on the Germans)*, Suhrkamp, Frankfurt, 1989.

Elster, J., *Nuts and Bolts for the Social Sciences*, Cambridge UP, Cambridge, 1993.

Ember, C.R. and Ember, M., War, socialization, and interpersonal violence, *Journal of Conflict Resolution*, 38, 620–646, 1994.

Enzensberger, H.M., *Oog in oog met de burgeroorlog (Eye to Eye with Civil War)*, De Bezige Bij, Amsterdam, 1994.

Esler, G., *The United States of Anger*, Penguin, London, 1997.

Etzioni, A., *The Moral Dimension. Toward a New Economics*, Free Press, New York, 1990.

Extra, J., *De machtsafstandsreductie–theorie van Mulder* (Mulder's power distance reduction theory), *Nederlands Tijdschrift voor Psychologie*, 33, 305–320, 1978.

Extra, J., *Mulder en de klassenstrijd* (Mulder and the class struggle), in Wiegman, O. and Wilke, H.A.M., (eds.), *Macht en beïnvloeding (Power and Influence)*, Van Loghum Slaterus, Deventer, 69–79, 1987.

Faber, M., *Novi Dani, nieuwe dagen. Oorlog en biografie in Banja Luka, Bosnië-Herzegovina (Novi Dani, New Days. War and Biography in Banja Luka, Bosnia Hercegovina)*, Aksant, Amsterdam, 2001.

Fasseur, C., *De weg naar het paradijs en andere Indische geschiedenissen (The Way to Paradise and Other Indonesian Histories)*, Bert Bakker, Amsterdam, 1995.

Fearon, J.D. and Laitin, D.D., Ethnicity, insurgency and civil war, *American Political Science Review*, 97, 75–90, 2003.

Flam, H., Fear, loyalty and greedy organizations, in Fineman, St., (ed.), *Emotion in Organizations*, Sage, London, 58–75, 1994.

Fletcher, J. *Violence and Civilization*, Polity Press, Cambridge, 1997.

Franke, H., *Geweldscriminaliteit in Nederland. Een historisch-sociologische analyse* (Violent crime in the Netherlands. A historical-sociological analysis), in Franke, H., Wilterdink, N. and Brinkgreve, C., (eds.), *Alledaags en ongewoon geweld* (Everyday and Unusual Violence), *Amsterdams Sociologisch Tijdschrift*, 18, 13–45, 1981.

Gagnon, V.P. Jr., Ethnic nationalism and international security: the case of Serbia, *International Security*, 19, 130–166, 1994–95.

Galtung, J., *Peace by Peaceful Means. Peace and Conflict, Development and Civilization*, Sage, London, 1996.

Gellner, E., *Nations and Nationalism*, Blackwell, Oxford, 1983.

George, S. and Sabelli, F., *Faith and Credit*, Penguin, Harmondsworth, 1994.

Gladwell, M., *The Tipping Point. How Little Things can Make a Big Difference*, Little, Brown and Co., Boston, 2000.

Glenny, M., *The Fall of Yugoslavia*, (New Ed.), Penguin, London, 1993.

Goldhagen, D.J., *Hitler's Willing Executioners: Ordinary Germans and the Holocaust*, Knopf, New York, 1996.

Goudsblom, J., *Het regime van de tijd (The Regime of Time)*, Meulenhoff, Amsterdam, 1997.

Gourevitch, Ph., *We Wish to Inform You that Tomorrow We will be Killed with our Families*, Farrar, Straus and Giroux, New York, 1998.

Granovetter, M., The strength of weak ties, *American Journal of Sociology*, 78, 1360–1380, 1973.

Guéhenno, J.M. de, *La fin de la démocratie (The End of Democracy)*, Flammarion, Paris, 1993.

Gurr, T.R., *Why Men Rebel*, Princeton UP, Princeton, 1970.

Haffner, S., *Anmerkungen zu Hitler (Observations on Hitler)*, Kindler, München, 1978.

Hall, J.R. *et al.*, *Apocalypse Observed. Religious Movements and Violence in North America, Europe, and Japan*, Routledge, London, 2000.

Hamilton, V. Lee and Sanders, J., Responsibility and risk in organizational crimes of obedience, in Staw, B.M. and Cummings, L.L., (eds.), *Research in Organizational Behavior*, JAI Press, Greenwich, 49–90, 1992.

Harrison, L.E. and Huntington, S.P., (eds.), *Culture Matters. How Values Shape Human Progress*, Basic Books, New York, 2000.

Hart, P. 't, *Groepsdenken in cruciale beslissingen, collectieve vermijding en over-optimisme* (Groupthink in crucial decision making: collective avoidance and overoptimism), *Psychologie en Maatschappij*, 14, 226–241, 1990.

Hatzfeld, J., *Une saison des machettes (A Season of Machetes)*, Eds. Du Seuil, Paris, 2003.

Heidenreich, J.G., *How to Prevent Genocide. A Guide for Policy Makers, Scholars, and the Concerned Citizen*, Praeger, Westport, 2001.

Helvacioglu, B., Globalization in the neighbourhood: from the nation-state to Bilkent Center, *International Sociology*, 15, 326–342, 2000.

Hersh, S.M., *Chain of Command*, HarperCollins, New York, 2004.

Hewstone, M. and Brown, R., (eds.), *Contact and Conflict in Intergroup Encounters*, Blackwell, Oxford, 1986.

Hobsbawm, E. and Ranger, T., *The Invention of Tradition*, Cambridge UP, Cambridge, 1984.

Hodson, R., Sekulic, D. and Massey, G., National tolerance in the former Yugoslavia, *American Journal of Sociology*, 99, 1534–1558, 1994.

Hofstede, G.H., *Cultures and Organizations. Software of the Mind*, McGraw-Hill, London, 1991.

Hofstede, G.H., Images of Europe, *Netherlands' Journal of Social Sciences*, 30, 63–82, 1994.

Hofstede, G.H., *Culture's Consequences. Comparing Values, Behaviors, Institutions and Organizations Across Nations*, Sage, London, 2001.

Hogg, M.A. and Abrams, D., *Social Identifications. A Social Psychology of Intergroup Relations and Group Processes*, Routledge, London, 1988.

Hoogerwerf, A., *Geweld in Nederland (Violence in the Netherlands)*, Van Gorcum, Assen, 1996.

Hooghe, L., Belgium. From regionalism to federalism, in Coakly, J., (ed.), *The Territorial Management of Ethnic Conflict*, (sec. and rev. edn), Frank Cass, London, 73–98, 2003.

Horowitz, D.L., *Ethnic Groups in Conflict*, University of California Press, Berkeley, 1985.

Horowitz, D.L., *The Deadly Ethnic Riot*, University of California Press, Berkeley, 2001.

Hudson, V.M. and Den Boer, A., A surplus of men, a deficit of peace, *International Security*, 26-4, 5–38, 2002.

Huntington, S., *The Clash of Civilisations and the Remaking of the World Order*, Simon and Schuster, New York, 2003 (first published 1996).

Inglehart, R. and Barker, W.E., Modernization, cultural change, and the persistence of traditional values, *American Sociological Review*, 65, 19–51, 2000.

Joris, L., *Dans van de luipaard (Dance of the Leopard)*, Meulenhoff, Amsterdam, 2001.

Juergensmeyer, J., *Terror in the Mind of God. The Global Rise of Religious Violence*, University of California Press, Berkeley, 2000.

Kaldor, M., *New and Old Wars. Organized Violence in a Global Era*, Polity Press, Cambridge, 1999.

Kaldor, M., *Global Civil Society. An Answer to War*, Polity Press, Cambridge, 2003.

Kaplan, R.D., *The Ends of the Earth. A Journey at the Dawn of the 21st Century*, Random House, New York, 1996.

Kaplan, J., (ed.), *Millennial Violence. Past, Present and Future*, Frank Cass, London, 2002.

Kaufmann, Ch., Possible and impossible solutions to ethnic civil wars, *International Security*, 20, 136–175, 1996.

Kaufman, S.J., Spiraling to ethnic war, *International Security*, 21, 108–138, 1996.

Kelley, M.J., *Restoring and Maintaining Order in Complex Peace Operations. The Search for a Legal Framework,* Kluwer, The Hague, 1999.

Kelman, H.C., Violence without moral constraint, *Journal of Social Issues*, 29, 29–61, 1973.

Kelman, H.C., Social-psychological dimensions of international conflict, in William Zartman, I. and Lewis Rasmussen J., (eds.), *Peacemaking in International Conflict. Methods & Techniques*, United States Institute of Peace, Washington D.C., 191–237, 2001.

Kelman, H.C. and Lee Hamilton, V., *Crimes of Obedience. Toward a Social Psychology of Authority and Responsibility*, Yale UP, New Haven and London, 1989.

Kets de Vries, M. and Miller, D., *The Neurotic Organization: Diagnosing and Changing Counterproductive Styles of Management*, Jossey-Bass, San Francisco, 1984.

Kets de Vries, M., *Leaders, Fools and Impostors. Essays on the Psychology of Leadership*, Jossey-Bass, San Francisco, 1993.

Kets de Vries, M., *Organizational Paradoxes. Clinical Approaches to Management*, (Second Ed.), Routledge, London, 1995.

Kinzer, S., *Crescent and Star. Turkey between Two Worlds*, Farrar, Straus and Giroux, New York, 2001.

Koonings, K. and Kruijt, D., (eds.), *Societies of Fear. The Legacy of Civil War, Violence and Terror in Latin America*, ZED Books, London and New York, 1999.

Kymlicka, W., *Politics in the Vernacular. Nationalism, Multiculturalism, and Citizenship*, Oxford UP, Oxford, 2001.

Labat, S., *L'Algérie dans la guerre (Algeria in War)*, Editions Complex, Paris, 1994.

Laitin, D.D., National revivals and violence, *European Journal of Sociology*, 36, 3–43, 1995.

Lake, D.A. and Rothchild, D., Containing fear. The origins and management of ethnic conflict, *International Security*, 21, 41–75, 1996.

Lam Both, P., *South Sudan: Forgotten Tragedy*, Calgary UP, Calgary, 2002.

Lammers, C.J., The organization of mass murder, *Organization Studies*, 16, 139–156, 1995.

Lammers, C.J., *Nederland als bezettende mogendheid 1648–2001 (The Netherlands as an Occupying Power)*, KNAW, Amsterdam, 2003.

Leistra, G. and Nieuwbeerta, P., *Tien jaar moord en doodslag in Nederland (Ten Years of Murder and Homicide)*, Prometheus, Amsterdam, 2003.

Lewis, B.L., *What Went Wrong? Western Impact and Middle Eastern Response*, Phoenix, London, 2002.

Lopreato, J., Authority relations and class conflict, in Lopreato, J. and Lewis, L., (eds.), *Social Stratification: A Reader*, Harper and Row, New York, 7–16, 1974.

Maduk Jot, J. and Hutchinson, S.E., Sudan's prolonged second civil war and the militarization of Nuer and Dinka ethnic identities, *Africa Studies Review*, 42, 125–145, 1999.

Maffesoli, M., *The Time of the Tribes*, Sage, London, 1996.

Mann, M., *The Dark Side of Democracy: Explaining Ethnic Cleansing*, Cambridge UP, Cambridge, 2, 2005.

135

McAdam, D., *et al.*, *Dynamics of Contention*, Cambridge UP, Cambridge, 2001.

McNamara, R.S., *In Retrospect. The Tragedy and Lessons of Vietnam*, Times Books, New York, 1995.

Mearsheimer, J.J., The false promise of international institutions, *International Security*, 19, 5–49, 1994–95.

Manor, J., The failure of political integration in Sri Lanka (Ceylon), *Journal of Commonwealth and Comparative Politics*, 17, 21–46, 1989.

Marwell, G., Oliver, P.E. and Prahl, R., Social networks and collective action: a theory of the critical mass (III), *American Journal of Sociology*, 94, 502–534, 1998.

Marx, G.T. and Wood, J.L., Strands of theory and research in collective behavior, *Annual Review of Sociology*, 1, 367–428, 1975.

Masuch, M., Vicious circles, *Administrative Science Quarterly*, 30, 14–33, 1985.

Masuch, M., The determinants of organizational harm, *Research in the Sociology of Organizations*, 9, 79–102, 1990.

Meijer, F., *Keizers sterven niet in bed (Emperors Do not Die in Bed)*, Atheneum, Amsterdam, 2001.

Meijer, F., *Gladiatoren. Volksvermaak in het Colosseum (Gladiators. Public Entertainment in the Colosseum)*, Atheneum, Amsterdam, 2003.

Melbin, M., Night as frontier, *American Sociological Review*, 43, 3–22, 1978.

Mennell, S., Short-term interests and long-term processes: the case of civilization and decivilization, in Goudsblom, J., Jones, E.L. and Mennell, St. (eds.), *Human History and Social Process*, University of Exeter Press, Exeter, 93–127, 1989.

Mennell, S., Decivilising processes: theoretical significance and some lines of research, *International Sociology*, 5, 205–223, 1990.

Mennell, St., *Norbert Elias, an Introduction*, Blackwell, Oxford, 1992.

Merton, R.K., *Social Theory and Social Structure*, (enlarged edn), Macmillan, New York, 1968.

Mertus, J., The impact of intervention on local human rights culture: a Kosovo case study, *Global Review of Ethnopolitics*, 1-2, 21–36, 2001.

Mestrovic, M., *The Balkanization of the West. The Confluence of Postmodernism and Postcommunism*, Routledge, London, 1994.

Meyer, J.W., Globalization. Sources and effects on national states and societies, *International Sociology*, 15, 233–248, 2000.

Milgram, S., Behavior study of obedience, *Journal of Abnormal and Social Psychology*, 67, 371–378, 1963.

Misra, A., *Afghanistan. The Labyrinth of Violence*, Polity Press, Cambridge, 2004.

Mulder, M., *Het spel om de macht. Over vergroting en verkleining van machtongelijkheid (The Power Game. About Enlargement and Reduction of Power Inequality)*, Boom, Meppel, 1978.

Muskens, G., *Hitler's gewillige beulen* (Hitler's willing executioners), *Facta*, 4, 7–9, 1996.

Nagatsuka, R., *I was a Kamikaze. The Knights of the Divine Wind*, New English Library, London, 1973.

Nisbett, R.E. and Cohen, D., *Culture of Honor. The Psychology of Violence in the South*, Westview Press, Boulder, 1996.

Ohnuki-Tierney, E., *Kamikaze, Cherry Blossoms, and Nationalisms*, University of Chicago Press, Chicago, 2002.

Opp, K.D., *Die Entstehung sozialer Normen (The Origin of Social Norms)*, Mohr Verlag, Tübingen, 1983.

Pamuk, O., The anger of the damned, *New York Review of Books*, 15 November, 2001.

Peters, K. and Richards, P., "Why we fight": voices of youth combatants in Sierra Leone, *Africa*, 68, 183–210, 1998.

Petter Gleditsch, N., Wallensteen, P., Erikson, M., Sollenberg, M. and Strand, H., Armed conflict 1946–2001: a new data set, *Journal of Peace Research*, 39, 615–637, 2002.

Popitz, H., *Phänomene der Gewalt (Manifestations of Violence)*, Mohr, Tübingen, 1999.

Port, M. van de, *Het einde van de wereld. Beschaving, redeloosheid en zigeunercafés in Servië (The End of the World. Civilization, Irrationality, and Gipsy Bars in Serbia)*, Babylon/de Geus, Amsterdam, 1994.

Power, S., *A Problem from Hell. America and the Age of Genocide*, Basic Books, New York, 2002.

Pyszczynski, T., Solomon, S. and Greenberg J., *In the Wake of 9/11. The Psychology of Terror*, American Psychological Association, Washington DC, 2003.

Radojčič-Kane, N., *Homecoming*, Four Walls Eight Windows, New York, 2002.

Ramdas, A., *In mijn vaders huis (In My Father's House)*, Mets, Amsterdam, 1993.

Rieff, D., *Slaughterhouse. Bosnia and the Failure of the West*, Vintage, London, 1995.

Ritzer, G., *The McDonalization of Society*, Pine Forge Press, Thousand Oaks, 1993.

Roberts, R., Interpretations of resurgent religion, *Theory, Culture and Society*, 13, 129–138, 1996.

Ryley Scott, G., *The History of Torture*, Bracken Books, London, 1995.

Saouïda, H., *La sale guerre (The Dirty War)*, Gallimard, Paris, 2001.

Schelling, Th.J., *Micromotives and Macrobehavior*, Norton, New York, 1978.

Schelling, Th.J., *Bloody Revenge. Emotions, Nationalism and War*, iUniverse, Lincoln, 2000.

Schreuder, O., *Sociale bewegingen, een systematische inleiding (Social Movements. A Systematic Introduction)*, van Loghum Slaterus, Deventer, 1981.

Schuyt, C.J.M., *Arbeidstijdverkorting en maatschappelijke orde* (Working time reduction and societal order), in Grumbkow, J. von and Godschalk, J.J., (eds.), *Sociale aspecten van arbeidstijdverkorting (Social Aspects of Working Time Reduction)*, Swets and Zeitlinger, Lisse, 165–174, 1984.

Schuyt, C.J.M., *Tweehonderd jaar stedelijk geweld* (Two hundred years of urban violence), *Delikt en Delinkwent*, 31, 785–791, 2001.

Scott, J.C., *Weapons of the Weak. Everyday Forms of Peasant Resistance*, Yale UP, New Haven and London, 1985.

Scott Bennett, D. and Stam, A.C., III, The duration of interstate wars, 1816–1985, *American Political Science Review*, 90, 239–257, 1996.

Scroggins, D., *Emma's War*, Pantheon Books, New York, 2002.

Segal, D.R. and Waldman, R.J., Multinational peacekeeping operations: background and effectiveness in Burk, J., (ed.), *The Military in New Times. Adapting Armed Forces to a Turbulent World*, Westview Press, Boulder, 1994.

Sells, M., *The Bridge Betrayed. Religion and Genocide in Bosnia*, University of California Press, Berkeley, 1998.

Sen., A., Democracy and its global roots, *The New Republic*, 6 October 2003.

Shaw, M., *Post-Military Society: War, Militarism and Demilitarization at the end of the Twentieth Century*, Temple University Press, Cambridge, 1991.

Silber, L. and Little, A., *The Death of Yugoslavia*, Penguin, London, 1996.

Singer, M. and Wildavsky, A., *The Real World Order. Zones of Peace, Zones of Turmoil*, Chatham House Publishers, Chatham, 1993.

Smith, Z.K., The impact of political liberalisation and democratisation on ethnic conflict in Africa: an empirical test of common assumptions, *Journal of Modern Africa Studies*, 38, 21–39, 2000.

Soeters, J., Governmental and administrative cultures in Belgium and the Netherlands: from divergence to convergence?, *International Review of Administrative Sciences*, 61, 265–278, 1995.

Soeters, J., Culture and conflict: an application of Hofstede's theory to the conflict in the former Yugoslavia, *Peace and Conflict. Journal of Peace Psychology*, 2, 233–244, 1996.

Soeters, J., The Dutch military and the use of violence, *Netherlands' Journal of Social Sciences*, 37, 24–37, 2001.

Soeters, J. and Twuyver, M. van, National and ethnic stereotyping in organizations, in Barfoot, C., (ed.), *Beyond Pug's Tour. National and Ethnic Stereotyping in Theory and Literary Practice*, RDC Books, Amsterdam, 495–510, 1997.

Sofsky, W., *Die Ordnung des Terrors: das Konzentrationslager (The Order of Terror. The Concentration Camp)*, Fischer, Frankfurt am Main, 1993.

Staub, E., Cultural–societal roots of violence. The examples of genocidal violence and of contemporary youth violence in the United States, *American Psychologist*, 51, 117–132, 1996.

Staw, B.M., Knee-deep in the big muddy: a study of escalating commitment to a chosen course of action, *Organizational Behavior and Human Performance*, 16, 27–44, 1976.

Stern, J., *Terror in the Name of God. Why Religious Militants Kill*, HarperCollins, New York, 2003.

Stiglitz, J., *Globalization and its Discontents*, Norton, New York, 2002.

Stouffer, S.A., *et al.*, *The American Soldier*. Vol I and II, Princeton UP, Princeton, 1949.

de Swaan, A., *In Care of the State. Health Care, Education and Welfare in Europe and the USA in the Modern Era*, Polity, Cambridge, 1988.

de Swaan, A., Perspectives for transnational social policy, *Government and Opposition. A Quarterly of Comparative Politics*, 27, 33–51, 1990.

de Swaan, A., De staat van wandaad. Over de vervagende grenzen tussen oorlogvoering en misdaadbestrijding (The State of Misdeed. About the waning borders between warring and crimefighting), *Twee stukken (Two Pieces)*, Het Spinhuis, Amsterdam, 1–14, 1994.

de Swaan, A., Widening circles of identification: emotional concerns in sociogenetic perspective, *Theory, Culture and Society*, 12, 25–39, 1995.

de Swaan, A., *De mensenmaatschappij. Een inleiding (Human Society. An Introduction)*, Bert Bakker, Amsterdam, 1996.

de Swaan, A., *Uitdijende kringen van desidentificatie: gedachten over Rwanda* (Widening circles of dysidentification: reflections on Rwanda), *Amsterdams Sociologisch Tijdschrift*, 24, 3–23, 1997.

de Swaan, A., *Dyscivilisatie, massale uitroeiing, en de staat* (Dyscivilization, mass extermination, and the state), *Amsterdams Sociologisch Tijdschrift*, 26, 289–301, 1999.

Tambiah, S.J., *Leveling Crowds. Ethnonationalist Conflicts and Collective Violence in South Asia*, University of California Press, Berkeley, 1996.

Teitler, G., *Toepassing van geweld. Sociologische essays over geweld, verzet en militaire organisatie (The Use of Violence. Sociological Essays on Violence, Resistance and Military Organization)*, Boom, Meppel, 1972.

Temmerman, E.de, *De doden zijn niet dood. Rwanda, een ooggetuigenverslag (The Dead are not Dead. Rwanda, an Eyewitness Report)*, Arbeiderspers, Amsterdam, 1994.

Tibi, B., *The Challenge of Fundamentalism. Political Islam and the New World Disorder*, (updated ed.), University of California Press, Berkeley, 2002.

Tilly, Ch., *Coercion, Capital and European States. AD 990–1990*, Blackwell, Cambridge, 1992.

Tilly, Ch., *The Politics of Collective Violence*, Cambridge UP, Cambridge, 2003.

Tishkov, V., Ethnic conflicts in the former USSR: the use and misuse of typologies and data, *Journal of Peace Research*, 36, 571–591, 1999.

Tishkov, V., *Chechnya: Life in a War-torn Society*, University of California Press, Berkeley, 2004.

Toffler, A. and Toffler, H., *War and anti-war. Survival at the Dawn of the 21st Century*, Bantam, New York, 1994.

Tomasic, D., Sociology in Yugoslavia, *American Journal of Sociology*, 47, 53–69, 1941.

Tomasic, D., The structure of Balkan society, *American Journal of Sociology*, 52, 132–140, 1946.

Triandis, H.C., *Individualism and Collectivism*, Westview Press, Boulder, 1995.

Turnbull, C.M., *The Mountain People*, Simon and Schuster, New York, 1972.

Ugresic, D., *De cultuur van leugens (The Culture of Lies)*, Nijgh & Van Ditmar, Amsterdam, 1995.

Vanhanen, T., Domestic ethnic conflict and ethnic nepotism: a comparative analysis, *Journal of Peace Research*, 36, 55–73, 1999.

Verweij, D., The dark side of obedience: the consequences of Hannah Arendt's analysis of the Eichmann case, *Professional Ethics*, 10, 143–158, 2002.

Vinken, H., Soeters, J. and Ester, P. (eds.), *Comparing cultures. Dimensions of Culture in a Comparative Perspective*, Brill, Leiden, 2004.

Vliert, E. van de, *et al.*, Temperature, cultural masculinity, and domestic political violence, *Journal of Cross-cultural Psychology*, 30, 291–314, 1999.

Volkov, V., Violent entrepeneurship in Post-Communist Russia, *Europe-Asia Studies*, 51, 741–754, 1999.

Voorhoeve, J.J.C., *Peace, Profits and Principles. A Study of Dutch Foreign Policy*, Martinus Nijhoff, The Hague, 1979.

Waal, F. de, *Good Natured. The Origins of Right and Wrong in Humans and Other Animals*, Harvard University Press, Cambridge, MA, 1996.

Wacquant, L.J.D., *Decivilisering en diabolisering. De transformatie van het Amerikaanse zwarte ghetto* (Decivilization and demonizing. The transformation of the American black ghetto), *Amsterdams Sociologisch Tijdschrift*, 24, 320–348, 1997.

Wallensteen, P. and Axell, K., Armed conflict at the end of the Cold War, *Journal of Peace Research*, 30, 331–346, 1993.

Wallensteen, P. and Sollenberg, M., The end of international war? Armed conflict 1989–1995, *Journal of Peace Research*, 33, 353–370, 1996.

Walzer, M., *Just and Unjust Wars. A Moral Argument with Historical Illustrations*, Basic Books, New York, 1992.

Weber, M., *The Sociology of Religion*, Methuen & Co Ltd, London, 1963.

Weinberg, L. and Pedahzur, A., *Political Parties and Terrorist Groups*, Routledge, London, 2003.

Wesseling, H.L., *Verdeel en heers. De deling van Afrika 1880–1914 (Divide and Rule. The Division of Africa 1880–1914)*, Bert Bakker, Amsterdam, 1992.

West, R., *Tito and the Rise and Fall of Yugoslavia*, Sinclair–Stevenson, London, 1994.

Wheatcroft, A., *Infidels. A History of the Conflict between Christendom and Islam*, Penguin, London, 2004.

Williams, B.F., A class act: anthropology and the race to nation across ethnic terrain, *Annual Review of Anthropology*, 18, 401–441, 1989.

Winslow, D. and Moelker, R., Chechnya, caught between globalization from above and globalization from below, in Kooiman D., *et al.* (eds.), *Conflict in a /Globalising World. Essays in Honour of Peter Kloos*, Van Gorcum, Assen, 211–228, 2002.

Wippler, R., *Nicht–intendierte soziale Folgen individueller Handlungen* (Unintended social consequences of individual acts), *Soziale Welt*, 29, 155–179, 1978.

Zakaria, F., *The Future of Freedom. Illiberal Democracy at Home and Abroad*, Norton, New York, 2003.

Zürcher, E.J., *Turkey. A Modern History*, I. B. Tauris, London, 2004.

Zwaan, T., Civilisering en decivilisering. Studies over staatsvorming en geweld, nationalisme en vervolging (Civilization and Decivilization. Studies on State Formation and Violence, Nationalism and Persecution), Boom, Amsterdam, 2001.

INDEX